THE MYSTERIOUS
WORLD OF CAVES

Publishers of the International Library

LIBRAIRIE ERNEST FLAMMARION—France
VERLAG J. F. SCHREIBER—Germany
(in association with Union Verlag, Stuttgart, and Oster. Bundesverlag, Vienna)
COLLINS PUBLISHERS—Great Britain
RIZZOLI EDITORE—Italy
FRANKLIN WATTS, INC.—United States of America

International Consultants

JEAN-FRANÇOIS POUPINEL—France
Ancien Elève Ecole Polytechnique
KLAUS DODERER—Germany
Professor, Frankfurt
MARGARET MEEK—Great Britain
Lecturer, Division of Language Teaching, Institute
of Education, University of London
FAUSTO MARIA BONGIOANNI—Italy
Professor of Education
at the University of Genoa
MARY V. GAVER—United States of America
Professor Emeritus, Graduate School of Library Science,
Rutgers University

International Editorial Board

HENRI NOGUÈRES
GERHARD SCHREIBER
JAN COLLINS
GIANNI FERRAUTO
HOWARD GRAHAM

INTERNATIONAL LIBRARY

ERNST BAUER

THE MYSTERIOUS WORLD OF CAVES

COLLINS · PUBLISHERS  FRANKLIN WATTS, INC.

London · Glasgow   New York

First Edition 1971
ISBN 0 00 100125 6 (*Collins*)
SBN 531 02102 5 (*Franklin Watts*)

ACKNOWLEDGMENTS

Cover: *Mairuel Grotto near Alava, northern Spain*, H. W. Franke: Frontispiece: *Main Hall, Schellenberg Ice Cave*, Anton Müller: Back end-papers, Kurt Krischke: Drawings and photographs, p. 6, Franke: 7, Bauer: 8 (2 bottom), Müller: 9 (top), Müller: 10 (3), Hermann Fay: 11, Helmut Frank: 12/13, 14, Fay: 15, Bauer: 16 (top), Jochen Hasenmayer: (bottom), Franke: 17, Bauer: 18 (top), Fay: (centre, left to right), Hasenmayer, Manfred Grohe (2): (bottom), Reutlinger General-Anzeiger: 19 (top), Grohe: (bottom), Bauer: 20, Hasenmayer: 21, 22 (top), Lebanese Tourist Office, Frankfurt: 22 (bottom), Bauer: 23, Franke: 24, Krischke: 24/25, Fay: 25, Krischke: 26 (left), Krischke: (top), Fay/Rücklin: 27 (top left), Müller: (bottom left), Frank: (right), Krischke: 28, Landesbildstelle Württemberg: 31, 32, Franke: 33 (2 top), Uribarri: (bottom), Professor Dr Herbert Kühm, Mainz: 34, Prähistorische Sammlungen, Ulm: 35 (top), Eugen Krautwasser: (bottom), 36, V-Dia-Verlag: 37, Professor Dr Herbert Kühm, Mainz: 38 (2), Uribarri: 39 (top), Krischke: (bottom), Spanish Tourist Office, Frankfurt: 40 (2), Bauer: 41, Landes-bildstelle Württemberg: 42 (left), Fay: (right), Bauer: 43 (right), Fay: 44/45 (top), Krischke: 44, 45 (bottom), Bauer: 46, Zentrale Farbbild-Agentur: 48, Bauer: 49 (top), Fay: (bottom), Herbert Hölker: 50, Frank: 51 (top), Fay: (bottom), Müller: 52, Fay: 53 (top), Krischke: (centre), Bauer: (bottom), Fay: 54 (top), Fay: (bottom), K. Riek: 55 (top), Fay: (bottom), Frank: 56, Fay: 57 (top), Fritz Schwäble: (bottom), Fay: 58 (top left), Bauer: (top right), Klaus Dobat: (bottom), Riek: 59 (2), Krischke: 60, Krischke/Dobat: 61, 62, Bauer: 63 (left), Krischke/Dobat/Schwoerbel: 63 (centre), Bauer: (right), Krischke/Dobat: 64, Franke: 65, Bauer: 66, Teichmann: 67, Bauer: 68 (top), Krischke/Stirn: (bottom), Bauer: 69 (top), Fay: (bottom), Bauer: 70, 71 (3), Bauer: 72, Wolfgang Krebs: 73 (top), Fay: (bottom left), Bauer: (bottom right), Ottmar: 74, Fay: 75, 76, Bauer: 77, Fay: 78 (top), F. Trapp-Bavaria: 78 (2 bottom), Bauer: 79 (top), Alfred Bögli: (bottom), Fay: 80, 81 (3), Bauer: 82, Franke: 84, Bauer: 85 (2 top), Bauer: (bottom), Bögli: 87, Bauer: 88 (4), Bauer: 89 (top), Krischke: (bottom), Bauer: 90, Müller: 91 (top left), V-Dia: (top right), Bauer: (centre), Bögli: (bottom), Krischke/Trimmel: 92, Müller: 93 (top), Müller: (bottom), Bauer: 94, 95, Bauer: 96 (top), Krischke/Wagner: 96 (bottom), Krischke: 97 (3), Bauer: 98, Fay: 99, Bauer: 100 (top), Ziegler: (bottom), Krischke: 101, Fay/Wagner: 102, Fay/Wagner: 103 (centre and right), Bauer: (left), Krischke: 104, Walter Sigl: 105, 106, Bauer: 107, Fay: 108 (top), Krischke/Franke: (bottom), Bauer: 109 (3), Sigl: 110 (top), Krischke: (bottom), Bauer: 111, Krischke: 112 (left), Bauer: (right), Krischke: 113, Bauer: 114, Bögli: 116 (top), Lebanese Tourist Office, Frankfurt: (bottom), Bauer: 117, 118, Müller: 119, Bögli: 120, Krischke: 121 (top), Krischke: (bottom), Bögli: 122, Müller: 123, Hasenmayer: 124 (top), Bögli: (bottom), Müller: 125 (2), Bauer: 126 (top), Bauer: (bottom), USIS: 127 (top), Bauer: (bottom), Müller.

Printed and bound in Great Britain by Jarrold & Sons Ltd., Norwich
Library of Congress Catalog Card Number: 70-153824

CONTENTS

CHAPTER 1

EXPLORATION UNDERGROUND

The challenge of caving

The geological formations known as caves are as old as the earth itself. The majority are made of limestone rocks, which have been traced back well over 300 million years. Others, formed by the action of wind, wave, lava and ice, may be even older. All of them hold secrets—secrets that must be prised from their depths—and then scientifically appraised and interpreted. From such evidence it has been possible to fill in many of the gaps in our knowledge concerning the age of the earth, its structure, its climate and its appearance millions of years ago. Geologists, studying the history, composition and development of the earth's crust, and hydrologists, who make a special study of water distribution on and below the earth's surface, rely extensively on the samples, photographs, maps and reports procured from caves. Such evidence is the responsibility of those who make the scientific study of caves their life's work. They are known as speleologists.

The caves hold other secrets as well—species of creatures of great antiquity, surviving links with some of the oldest forms of life on earth; and relics dating back to the dawn of human existence, such as the bones, skulls and skeletons of cave men, together with examples of their art and culture. Thus the palaeontologists, who study the origins of plant and animal life, and the archaeologists, who investigate the history of man and civilization from existing remains, also have important stakes in the field of speleological research.

Caving, whether as a hobby or a science, is a relatively recent activity, not much more than a century old. Regarded purely as a sport or recreation, it offers the challenges and provides the thrills and joys that others derive from mountaineering or underwater exploration. In its

Left: the wonder of the subterranean world. The Erlach Cave in Lower Austria was only recently discovered. Although relatively small, it contains a varied display of stalactites.

Caving equipment must be severely practical. Helmet, lamp, overalls, stout boots and waistlength are among essential clothes and accessories. The cameraman shooting this television film in the Bauerloch Cave is dressed exactly like the cavers.

A carbide (acetylene) lamp.

more expert forms, it combines some of the skills needed for both these activities. Yet the dedicated caver, potholer or spelunker (he owns to many names) looks for more than the satisfaction of arduous and sometimes dangerous physical achievement. For him there is always the chance and hope of a new discovery, a new point of departure. In this mysterious and exciting underground world, some can claim to have probed farther and deeper than others, but nobody can ever claim to have gone farthest or deepest. There are no absolutes in this realm. It is this perpetual lure of the uncharted and unknown which drives the caver on. So much still waits to be found.

There are many excellent books on caves and caving, from the classic firsthand narratives of men such as Casteret and Tazieff to the practical guides, written by those who have devoted their leisure and often their working lives to speleology. This book attempts a more general survey of the subject. It deals with caving procedures and techniques, but in addition to supplying information it aims to convey, both to the enthusiast and the uninitiated, something of the awe-inspiring wonder

Acetylene lamps have a long life, cast a bright light and may, if desired, be home-made. Left: the Angerloch Cave. Right: the Great Spielberg Cave.

and beauty of this vast subterranean world.

Subterranean grandeur

No written descriptions can really do justice to the underground world of caves—the domed caverns, gleaming walls, raging river torrents, crystal-pure lakes and fantastic decorative formations. It is a world of breathtaking beauty, an endless maze of twisting passages and crevices, often barely wide enough for a human body to wriggle through, sometimes blocked by rocks or water, then unexpectedly opening up into larger caves from which new networks extend. Venturing into such unexplored regions, even the most experienced caver is faced with new challenges, new dangers, at every turn. Sometimes the end result is frustration and disappointment; but fortune may lead him farther and deeper into subterranean zones where no human has ever set foot. This alone is sufficient reward, yet there is always the unexpressed hope that he may light upon something even more momentous, evidence perhaps of former habitation —skeletons, rock paintings, primitive tools and artefacts—a new Lascaux or Altamira.

Thanks to the pioneers of speleology and the many enthusiasts who have since followed in their footsteps, less adventurous folk have also been given the opportunity to share the wonder of this unknown world. Underground railways carry them in comfort miles into the heart of cave systems, while boats ferry them along streams and over the placid surface of lakes hundreds of feet below ground. Guided tours of the spectacular show caves of the world bring in welcome revenue and rival the traditional natural and manmade marvels above the surface.

Potholers, spelunkers and the like welcome the chance to display the splendours of the underground landscape to such visitors, for it helps to explain why they were attracted by caves in the first place. Yet few people who gaze in admiration round these caverns of rock and ice, with their romantic and evocative names—Grand Canyon, Great Cathedral, Alhambra, Crystal Lake, Roaring River—can imagine the physical hardship and danger which had to be endured to make it all possible.

The element of luck

Many of the world's most famous caves were discovered by sheer accident. The Nebelhöhle, or Cavern of Mist, in Liechstenstein was found by a hunter in the early 16th century, while pursuing a deer. In 1809, a bear apparently led an American hunter to the mouth of the immense Mammoth Cave in Kentucky. In 1901, a cowboy named Jim White was attracted by what appeared to be a huge column of smoke emerging from a rock cleft. It proved to be a swarm of bats around the entrance to the Carlsbad Cavern, the largest cave in the world. A small girl, wandering away from her father, discovered the fabulous prehistoric paintings at Altamira; and a dog, falling into a cleft, led a group of boys to the equally sensational painted caves of Lascaux. Similar accidental discoveries have been recorded all over the world.

The initial finding of a new cave may have its element of luck, but the subsequent stages of penetration and exploration demand perseverance and skill. Although men have been going down caves for hundreds of years—the celebrated Postojna Caves were supposedly visited by Dante nearly 700 years ago—serious caving dates from the 19th century.

The flame of the carbide lamp throws out welcome warmth during rest periods.

Most of the significant European discoveries occurred toward the end of that century and in the years preceding the first World War, as rambling and caving clubs and societies were formed to accommodate the growing numbers of enthusiasts. The emphasis was on breaking new ground rather than setting up records. In fact, the depth record of 1,079 feet, set up in the Grotta di Trebiciano in 1841, was not surpassed for 65 years when cavers reached 1,293 feet in the Nidlenloch in Switzerland. And whereas the record was broken four times during the century following the original Italian feat of 1841, it was smashed no less than six times during the decade after the second World War.

What every caver should know

Investigation of a fairly level, dry cave can be undertaken by anyone with sufficient energy and curiosity, armed with little more than a torch and wearing sensible clothing. But where more difficult caves are involved, and certainly where there are vertical shafts known as potholes,

A lamp attached to the forehead is always practical, casting a beam straight ahead.

9

Wire rope or electron ladders are often used in caves with vertical shafts. The rungs are made of aluminium tubing and several ladders can be linked with karabiners to give additional length.

a greater degree of preparation, plus some practical knowledge and experience, are essential. And the scientific exploration of caves lying many hundreds of feet below ground calls for careful planning and the most up-to-date equipment.

Many excellent guidebooks are obtainable on caving and potholing, and the beginner will obviously need to consult one or more of these. A few general principles and basic rules, however, may be mentioned here, bearing in mind that such regulations and procedures are very flexible, to be interpreted and adapted according to individual requirements and cave conditions.

The importance of teamwork

Nevertheless, there are certain golden rules which should apply to all amateur potholers and spelunkers, even for short expeditions. The first rule is never to attempt to go it alone. This is all very well for a Casteret, but not for a beginner. Always travel in company, or, best of all, join a caving club. Members of these will hardly need to be told what to do, but preliminary work will include a thorough survey of the terrain to be explored (if not already known), the obtaining of necessary permission from local farmers and landowners, and the selection of a cave or system well within the capability of every member of the team. Caves are habitually graded from "easy" to "severe" and "supersevere" (or similar equivalents), and progression from one to another should be gradual. A careful check should be made of weather prospects for the period one intends to remain underground—a sudden heavy rainstorm can turn a placid stream into a racing torrent—and information left regarding destination and estimated time of return. A generous

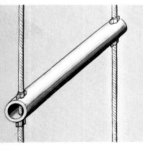

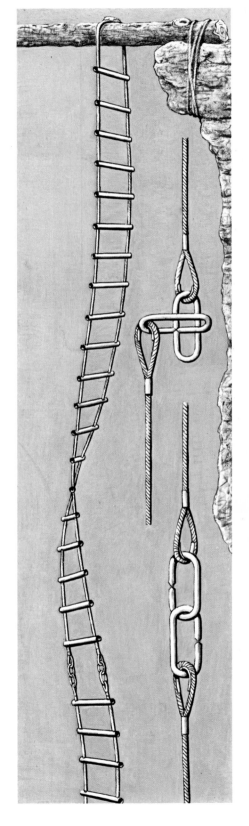

margin of error should be allowed in such reckoning, for the passing of time underground is a deceptive business, as any experienced caver will testify and may have learned to his cost.

Sensible clothing

It must be self-evident that adequate personal and team equipment should be carried in order to cope with the contingencies of such an expedition. Clothing cannot always be a casual matter of old overalls, a pair of leakproof shoes and some kind of head protection, although for small caves these may suffice. Wherever there is an element of risk, the choice of clothing needs more careful thought.

The mean temperature in most caves (excluding ice caves) is between 46° and 48°F (8°–9°C), though some can be markedly cooler. Clothes must therefore be warm and comfortable, though not too bulky to impede movement. Woollen underwear is always advisable, for the fibres retain warm air. Next should come a shirt—flannel is better than cotton or nylon—and several light sweaters, easily discarded if necessary. Trousers should be of sufficiently tough material to stand up to prolonged crawling, and loose enough to allow free movement. To cover everything, the best garment is a boiler suit, not too tightly fitting and not cluttered with too many pockets.

A boiler suit will provide reasonable protection in all but the wettest caves, where a rubber exposure suit is essential. These come in two types, the dry and the wet suit. The former is made of thin rubber, convenient to wear under an overall or boiler suit, but not designed specifically for caving. It has the disadvantage of being easily punctured. Better,

There are right and wrong ways of using ladders. The correct method is to grip alternately from in front and behind.

though more expensive, is the wet suit, of the type used by water-skiers and frogmen, made of Neoprene foam rubber, very close-fitting and worn without any clothing underneath. It retains body heat effectively, is ventilated by a zip, and will not leak even if slightly torn.

Footwear must also be carefully considered. Two pairs of woollen socks are a good idea, one to go under and one over the boiler suit.

Many cavers prefer a pair of knee-length gaiters. But there is no argument over the last item—a stout pair of boots, either with leather uppers and rubber, cleated "commando" soles, or reinforced with tricouni nails or clinkers. Nails afford a better grip on slippery surfaces but can damage ropes and ladders, so that some clubs prohibit their use. Metal toe caps are useful, but whatever type is chosen, boots must be sturdy and comfortable and should be fitted with eyelets rather than hook laces.

Even for caves of moderate difficulty, a helmet is essential, to protect the head against low roofs and falling rocks. There are many types on the market, but the important point is that it should be fairly lightweight—plastic and fibreglass are the most common—and that the headband and chinstrap should fit snugly, but not too tightly. The only really necessary attachment is a lamp bracket, with cable clip.

Essential equipment

All personal items of equipment should be neatly packed into a canvas haversack, which can be carried or slung over the shoulder. Individual articles can be waterproofed with plastic or packed into airtight tins with screw tops. For an underground bivouac, more equipment and food will obviously be required, but it is always wise to take more than you are likely to need. Good energy-providing foods include chocolate, barley sugar and boiled sweets, glucose tablets, dates, nuts and raisins, fruit cake, etc. Caving is also thirsty work, but do not trust natural cave water, which may be polluted. A flask of water, some fruit juice and a thermos of tea or coffee are "musts".

A small first-aid kit, with a roll of gauze, adhesive dressings, aspirins and antiseptic ointment, should be packed separately in a waterproof tin. Other personal accessories should include a notebook and pencil, or plastic sheet and chinagraph crayon. Watches must be waterproof and a penknife and compass are always handy. A whistle should be carried on a cord round the neck or fastened and tucked into a chest pocket. Finally—and this is an essential, not an optional, piece of equipment—every caver must carry a waistlength, a rope five-eighths of an inch thick and eight feet or more long, made of nylon or one of the newer manmade fibres. This is looped round the waist and is used for belaying or in conjunction with other lengths to

The Gouffre Pierre Saint-Martin is the deepest cave in the world. The entrance to this vast subterranean labyrinth is in Spain but the system extends into France. The immense height of the caverns may be appreciated by comparing them with Strasbourg Cathedral.

High points in caves can be reached by means of interconnecting poles which make up a so-called maypole. It is held in position by guylines.

form an emergency rope. Small metal snaplinks known as karabiners should also be carried, as they are vital in any form of normal cave work. Chest harnesses, though bulky, are also recommended for particularly dangerous descents.

Lighting is another important consideration in caving. Matches and candles (as used by all the early speleologists) and pocket torches are all useful, but unsatisfactory for continuous and penetrating work. For main lighting the choice lies between electric lamps (with wet or dry cell batteries) and carbide or acetylene lamps. The modern miner's type of headlamp, affixed to the helmet, is popular, though it is rather heavy and requires regular charging and maintenance. One bulb supplies about ten hours of main beam lighting or some thirty hours of pilot beam illumination. Dangers of wet cell batteries include alkaline leaks, which can cause serious burns.

The carbide helmet lamp, with its flint and wheel ignition, is cheap and convenient to handle. It is comprised of two sections, the water from the upper container dripping down on the calcium carbide in the lower portion to produce the acetylene gas. The lamp throws out a soft, powerfully diffused light and burns, without refilling, for between three and five hours. Refills and jet cleaners must be carried and the white porridge-like residue taken back to the surface in airtight containers, since used carbide is harmful to animal life. Among the disadvantages of carbide lamps are that they are useless in water, burn poorly when tipped on their sides and must be kept well clear of ropes and rope ladders. Whichever type of main lighting is chosen, some form of spare illumination must also be taken along.

Ropes, ladders and other tackle

The basic items of group equipment for caving and potholing are ropes and ladders, and one experienced team member should be appointed to supervise this and other tackle. Cavers still argue fiercely about the merits and disadvantages of different types of rope. Although a certain amount of climbing has to be done, the essential requirement of a potholing rope is strength rather than elasticity. Nylon is preferable to natural hemp, which has a tendency to stiffen when wet, rot and even snap. Nylon is light, stands up well to water, is unaffected by chemicals and, with a one-and-a-quarter-inch diameter, has a satisfactory breaking strain of at least 4,000 pounds. Its elasticity, however, makes some climbing techniques difficult, it is highly inflammable and it tends to accumulate dirt. Other manmade fibres, such as Ulstron and Courlene, have the advantages of nylon, without its drawbacks.

Rope ladders are rarely used nowadays, for the lightweight wire or electron ladders, first introduced in France, are safer and less cumbersome. They can be purchased in lengths of 25–30 feet or more, or, given the necessary patience and skill, may be homemade. Extreme care must be taken to ensure that galvanized steel wire and aluminium alloy rungs can stand the requisite strains—over 1,100 pounds in the case of the wire and 850 pounds for the rungs.

Where excessive depths are to be plumbed, more sophisticated equipment, such as the wire-rope winch, may have to be used. Any form of descent by single rope is highly risky, and even experts have met with fatal accidents. The experienced caver, Marcel Loubens, using a wire rope only one-fifth of an inch in diameter, fell to his death in the course of his return ascent in the Gouffre de la Pierre Saint-Martin, in 1952, and three Italian cavers were killed similarly in 1965.

Supplementary climbing equipment includes pitons—steel pegs

The water in this underground lake is 48°F (9°C) but the diver is thoroughly protected and insulated by his exposure suit as he wades through the spring which is its source.

with a ring at the end for fixing karabiners—hammers, for knocking them into horizontal or vertical fissures, rawlbolts and expansion bolts. The last are made of aluminium

and are increasingly replacing the standard climbers' pitons. Etriers, or short lengths of ladder, are sometimes used for short pitches, and expanding stemples (wedges of metal) can be substituted for ladders across narrow passages or for hoisting loads. Single-sheaf pulleys are helpful for hauling equipment, and for rock faces where it is difficult to fix pitons or expansion bolts, a scaling pole (known as a maypole) is indispensable. This is made of aluminium alloy tubing, similar to that used for scaffolding, the pieces being joined together by clamps. The top is equipped with ring bolts, to which are attached the wire ladder being hoisted into position and the lifeline pulley.

Digging implements such as crowbars, chisels, hammers, shovels, trenching tools and buckets, are vital if a new cave system is being explored. Pumps are needed where water is to be extracted from a flooded cave, and for any expedition where cavers are likely to be working at a distance from one another or risk being separated by rocks and water, field telephones are a tremendous asset, both to communicate below ground and to maintain contact with those above.

Modern communication methods include magnetic induction systems, with a coil signalling vertically up to the surface from a point within a cave. This can also be used to locate points on the surface above caves, for survey accuracy improvement and for pinpointing the position of shafts for access or rescue. There is also guided radio, using normal radio transmitter/receivers near a guide wire—an insulated wire running through the cave and earthed at both ends.

Where lakes are liable to be encountered, many clubs favour carrying inflatable rubber dinghies —to take two cavers—together with life jackets. And if deep cave diving is to be attempted, by fully trained experts only, the most modern underwater equipment, including breathing apparatus, wet suit, goggles, flippers, watertight lamps and depth gauges, is obviously vital.

Training and technique

As in any sport or hobby, success depends, in the last resort, on individual ability, knowledge and skill. Caving is especially heavy in its demands on temperament and character. It calls for patience, discipline, resourcefulness and imagination. There is no place underground for the loner, the risk-taker and the exhibitionist. Danger must be minimized, for injury can not only hinder progress but also imperil the lives of the whole team. The expedition leader must be well aware of the needs and capabilities of his colleagues. Novices must be closely attached to more experienced cavers and each team member should be quite certain of his particular function and task.

One golden rule underground is— take your time. Progress, even in straightforward sections, should be steady and controlled, never rapid and impulsive. This principle is especially important when special difficulties are encountered. To keep

Above left: progress is possible as long as there is clear air between the cave roof and the water surface; but caving is not recommended to anyone suffering from claustrophobia.

Below left: cave streams can often be comfortably negotiated in an inflatable rubber boat, though for exploratory work a crew of two is essential. This picture was taken in the Križna Jama, Yugoslavia.

Magnesium torches have the advantage of burning under water and give out a brilliant light.

A siphon, formed when the cave roof descends to water level, is best negotiated either by a quick duck or dive, provided its extent is known.

calm in all circumstances is more than half the battle. To panic is to court danger.

The complete caver must nevertheless learn to master certain techniques, none of which can be taught in books alone. No matter how many sets of rules have been pored over, the reality, when it comes, never quite tallies with the theory. Confidence only arrives with experience—the first vertical descent, the first squeeze through a narrow fissure, the first ledge traversed, the sight of the sky again after a successful expedition. Soon instinct and acquired skills merge imperceptibly until technique is taken for granted and the real pleasure and excitement begin.

Horizontal techniques are soon learned, for they involve no more than the intelligent and economical use of the body. As the cave roof

Four students, trapped for three days by a flood in the Falkenstein Cave, were rescued by divers who had to swim through a siphon, carrying blankets packed in tin boxes.

becomes gradually lower, an upright stance gives way to a stooping walk, then to a crouching gait. This can be a tiring method of making progress and some prefer to walk on all fours, monkey-fashion, holding haversack in mouth. Crawling on hands and knees may be necessary in some passages but kneeling is not advisable, leading as it can to painful scratches, cuts and bruises. The real problems begin when the roof descends to within a couple of feet of the floor. Now it is a question of lying quite flat and crawling forward, pushing one's kit ahead with the hands. Where there is enough height, a sideways crawl may be possible, lying first on the outside of one leg and then the other, and using one arm to pull the body forward. This is a variation of the flat-out crawl, with body prone. But when the gap narrows to a foot or so, there is no alternative but to wriggle forward, inches at a time.

Inevitably, cavers are sometimes faced with the narrowest of gaps, through which the body can only just fit. Such a passage is known as a squeeze, and it may be complicated by sloping up or down, and twisting in different directions. Obviously, some bodies will not fit through a really narrow passage, whatever technique is employed, so it must be assumed that the caver is reasonably slim and supple. For a squeeze, the body has to be compressed, with the widest parts—shoulders, hips and buttocks—accommodated to the broader sections of passage. Where the tunnel is horizontal, it is best to proceed head first on the stomach, though there may be sections more easily negotiated on the side or back. But where a passage slopes downward, or if it has not been probed previously, it may be dangerous to tackle it head first. It is largely a matter of instinct

and practice. The body is surprisingly flexible but if, as may well happen, one gets stuck, the rule once more is "Don't panic". Relaxing the entire body is vital, for struggling only makes things worse. A gentle push or pull, a short period of rest, or even just a few quiet words of encouragement, will probably do the trick.

Another problem frequently encountered in lateral travel is water. Apart from lakes and rivers, the most formidable barrier is the sump, a water trap which may signify the end of a cave. If it merely submerges a short section of passage, it may be possible to wade through or duck below the surface, holding one's breath. But if it is longer, in which case it is known as a siphon, other techniques will be required, either swimming or pulling oneself through with a guide wire. Neither method should be used without proper supervision and preparation. Underground water must always be treated with great respect, the flood level being watched continuously, and a retreat beaten if there is any doubt whatsoever.

Going down and coming up

For vertical descents down potholes, the safest and most popular method is by ladder, especially the electron ladder already described. The first step is to rig the ladder to a safe anchorage or belay, preferably a heavy rock or boulder, but failing that a length of crowbar driven into the rock. Expansion bolts and pitons should only be used if there are no alternatives. Electron ladders are joined together by C-links, which are also fastened to the belay wire. A few rungs are left to overlap the top of the pitch and the ladder is paid out gently until it reaches the bottom of the shaft.

A caver enjoys a hot cup of tea during an expedition.

Air bubbles at the surface of the spring pool indicate that the diver is on his way up.

With the ladder properly in position, preparations can now proceed for sending down the first climber. Before anything else is done, the lifeline must be firmly fixed. Another experienced member of the team takes up his position at the head of the ladder. If necessary, his feet can be wedged against a rock for added security. He then attaches one end of the lifeline rope (which is at least twice the length of the ladder) to a separate belay point, either with or without the aid of a sling. The other

Some of the equipment used by the cave diver Jochen Hasenmayer.

end of the rope is then attached to the climber, using a karabiner or tying on with a bowline and two half hitches.

The lifeliner now takes in the slack and provides either a waist or shoulder belay. The former is the more common method, with the rope going round the lifeliner's waist. Alternatively, the rope returning from the climber is passed under the lifeliner's arm, across his back and over the opposite shoulder.

The hand nearer to the climber now begins to pay out rope at the same speed as the climber moves down the ladder. The other hand (with a twist of rope encircling the wrist) is employed in controlling the rope by varying the amount of friction on the body. Thus he is easily able to take the strain of a possible fall without any sense of effort.

The climber places his arms round the ladder, gripping the rungs from behind. He places his feet alternately on the rungs, the toe of one boot on the front of one rung, the heel of the other boot round the back of the rung below. This helps the ladder to hang steadily and vertically, without swinging away from him. Where the ladder is flat against a rock face, both feet must be placed at the front, and pushed away with arms and instep or twisted sideways. Care must at all times be taken to keep the body vertical and close to the ladder. If the body is allowed to bend backwards, the ladder may swing dangerously.

In case of trouble, or while resting, the potholer can clip his karabiner to the side of the ladder. Use of his whistle will also give unambiguous instructions to the lifeliner—one for "stop", two for "up" or "take in", three for "down" or "pay out". Tugs on the rope can be employed if the whistle cannot be heard.

With the first man down, the rest can follow, and the lifeline re-rigged from below. The last man, however, should be double lifelined with a pulley or karabiner fixed to a belay at the head of the ladder, but controlled from the foot of the shaft. All equipment is lowered by rope, using knots and karabiners.

Coming up is always more difficult than going down, but the same principles and techniques apply. The best method of getting the ladder up again is to fix a rope to the bottom end and to haul it out from above as the last man ascends. He can make sure that it does not get caught or entangled on a projection.

There are other methods of des-

Floodlights illuminate the underground river in Lebanon's Jeita Cave.

A giant stalagmite in the Jeita Cave, ten miles north of Beirut.

Divers returning from an underwater cave.

Various techniques are nowadays adopted, the oldest way being to lower oneself by a double rope from the belay point, passing it under the thighs, over the chest and round the opposite shoulder, and using the back as a brake. A better method is to make the waistlength into a sling for the back and thighs and attach it to the double rope with a karabiner, thus enabling the climber to slide down the rope or walk down the pitch. This method cannot be used on the ascent, so that the ladder must be rigged beforehand. Alternatively, the caver can use the prusiking technique. The feet are placed in loops or stirrups, attached to the climbing rope with special prusik knots. These slide upwards as the feet move up alternately, but remain tight and secure under the body weight. This, however, is a single rope method, with all the attendant dangers, and new techniques are being examined which may reduce the risks of both ascent and descent.

Other established methods include the use of winches, either hand operated or power driven, and, for short, dry pitches, standard climbing techniques. For steeper ascents, cavers have to resort to the maypole and ladder method. Once safely underground, however, other climbing skills may be needed. The most experienced climber will take the lead in an ascent, if necessary securing himself with running belays. Once at the top of a pitch, he attaches his lifeline to a boulder or other belay point and assists the others up in approved rock-climbing fashion. But additional care must be taken underground because of the wet and sticky surfaces of cave walls, and at no time can lifelines be discarded.

Narrow chimneys or rock faces close together can sometimes be

cent and ascent by the use of ropes alone, the former being known as abseiling, the latter as prusiking. Both should be attempted only by really skilled cavers. Abseiling, or roping down, enables vertical rock faces to be negotiated very rapidly.

climbed by straddling the opposite walls and pulling oneself up by handholds. In narrower chimneys, the back may be wedged against one wall and the feet against the other, so that the body is gradually edged upwards. For traversing—that is, horizontal rock-climbing along or between walls above the floor of a passage—the lifeliner, securely be-

In Yugoslavia's Križna Jama, dripstone growths often impede progress and boats must be carried over barriers.

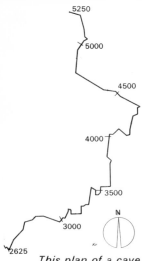

This plan of a cave recently filled by water demonstrates the close link between the cave pattern and natural geological faults.

layed, attaches a series of running belays as he progresses, with pitons, short loops known as belay lengths, and karabiners. The other members of the team, suitably linked together, can then use this rope as a handline, attaching themselves to it by karabiners from their waistlengths as they move along the ledge.

Ice and water

Ice caves naturally call for specialized equipment and climbing techniques, with axes and crampons to chip away the ice and hack out safe footholds. Wet caves too, where streams, rivers and lakes are the main features, call for completely different methods and aids. Faced by an unexpected siphon, even the most experienced swimmer is helpless. Further progress can only be attempted by experienced divers, who are often called upon to rescue cavers trapped by sudden floods and rising waters. In February 1964, for example, four students were trapped in the Falkenstein Cave in the Swabian Alps after a sudden thawing of winter snow. They were marooned for three days before being rescued by divers.

Standard deep diving equipment includes a wet suit, a self-contained breathing apparatus, a helmet with fixed lights, and of course a secure and easily manipulated safety link with a companion. Solo dives can be suicidal. All the more remarkable, therefore, to consider Norbert Casteret's astounding feat in 1922 when he dived unclothed, and without a companion, into a siphon in the Montespan Grotto. He carried only matches and candles and had no accessory air supply. His daring dive led him to discover priceless rock drawings and clay models of extinct animals.

Nowadays, compressed air has largely superseded the oxygen cylin-der, and certainly for deep dives, compressed air systems (including aqualungs) are essential. Where depths of 75 feet or more are involved, the diver is subjected, as in the ocean, to tremendous pressure. He risks being overcome by the "bends", a feeling of weightlessness which may lead to unconsciousness and even drowning. Equally there is the danger of coming up too rapidly, which can also result in severe muscular pain, partial paralysis and perhaps death. It is obvious, therefore, that cave diving requires very special training and considerable personal courage.

The world distance record for a cave dive is at present held by Jochen Hasenmayer, who, in the summer of 1970, swam 2,400 feet from his base in the de Balme caves of south east France, emerging in a superb stalactite-filled cavern.

Cave surveying

Surveying and mapping are vital, though somewhat uncomfortable, jobs in any exploration of a new cave system. Information has to be conveyed about the dimensions, extent and general structure of the cave, its underground rivers and its relationship to physical features above the surface. The conventional surveying methods, with precise sighting instruments and poles, can only be used in large chambers and straight passages. Elsewhere it is mainly a matter of gauging distances

The passages of even the largest caves are not arbitrary in direction but follow the basic geological structure of neighbouring terrain, as this picture of Spain's Ojo Guareña shows.

Palomera
Doline

Corneja
Cave

Tremp river

A block-diagram of the Blautopf, a spring in the Swabian Alps. The waters of a huge flooded cave rise to the surface here.

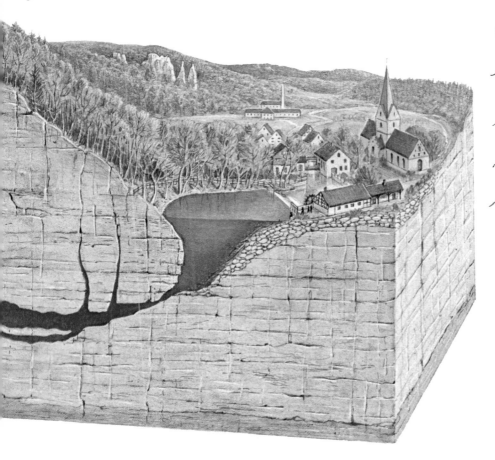

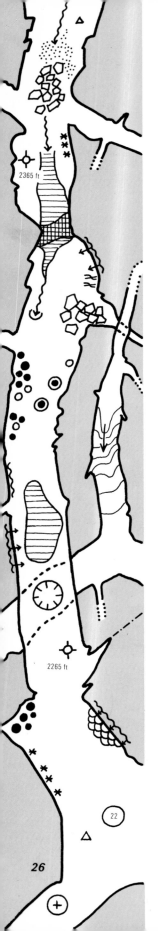

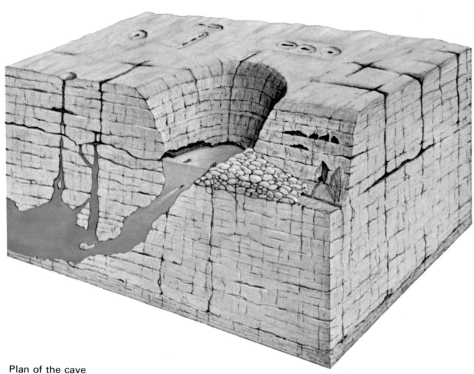

Plan of the cave

The water in the Vaucluse Cave near Avignon is so deep that it has so far defied all the efforts of divers to plumb it.

with special non-magnetic tape, taking horizontal directions with a compass, and measuring vertical angles or gradients with a device known as a clinometer. In difficult conditions underground it is generally possible to do little more than jot down such readings, making notes of additional features such as water courses, lakes, springs, shafts, bridges, etc. All these, as well as mud, sand, stalactites, stalagmites and so forth, are represented by conventional symbols. The filling in of detail and the close study and interpretation is done at the surface.

The most important information to be recorded on the spot, as faithfully as conditions permit, relates to distances, dimensions (height can sometimes be measured with a simple balloon), compass bearings and angles of slopes. As in other scientific fields, new instruments are continually being devised to provide easier and more accurate readings. One such piece of equipment is the Austrian "Xavermeter", which gives distance, direction and angle of incline in a single reading.

Cave photography

Sketches and photographs are also an invaluable aid to surveying. Cine-photography underground is a wasteful and highly expensive process, so that still photography, whether in colour or black-and-white, remains standard procedure. No absolutely ideal camera for cave conditions has so far been developed, and an inexpensive 35-mm camera, with interchangeable lenses, is normally as good as anything. It is very much a matter of preference, but photographic accessories must include a tripod and adequate lighting equipment.

Flashbulbs and electronic flash are the best lighting methods for underground use. Both have their advantages and disadvantages, the former being safer and more powerful, the latter heavier to transport but cheaper to operate after the initial capital cost, and with a much shorter flash duration. More sophisticated devices, operating synchronized multiple-flash systems, are of course more expensive, require ex-

The drawings in the margin, left, show some of the symbols used to prepare a cave map. The meanings of the various symbols are given in the margin, right.

Shafts that descend obliquely, such as these in the Great Spielberg Cave, are difficult to survey.

 Main surveying point

 2265 ft — Height above sea level

 Contour lines

 Direction of gradient

 Height of cave roof (feet)

−*136* +*7* — Relative differences in height

 Lower and upper cave passageway

 Eccentrics

 Internal shaft

 Chimney

 Rockfall

 Loam, sand

 Stalagmite

 Stalactite

 Pillar

 Sinter basin

 Sinter layer

 Glacier sediment water

 Lime crystals

 Swallow hole of a stream

Cave stream

 Siphon

 Percolating water

pert advice, but give excellent results.

Care must also be taken in choosing films and the decision may depend on whether slides or positive colour prints are desired. Films are available for use either in daylight or artificial light, and both types can be used underground with suitable filters. But as with ordinary photography, it often requires a certain amount of experiment before one hits on the film which gives utmost sharpness, tone contrast and colour fidelity.

CHAPTER 2

THE BURIED PAST

Endurance records

In January 1969, two French speleologists, Jacques Chabert and Philippe Englander, emerged from the Ollivier Cave near Nice. They had been living in the cave for almost five months, carrying out an experiment to test the possible effect, both on body and mind, of an enforced underground existence. Since the men conducted their tests separately, they did not even have the comfort of each other's company. With no means of measuring the passage of time, normal hours, days and weeks had absolutely no meaning for them. Indeed, their "days" often lasted as much as 48 hours, during which time they found that they needed only twelve hours sleep.

Six months later a Yugoslav caver performed a similar experiment on his own. On June 24 1969, Milutin Veljkovic disappeared into the Samar Cave. After giving a brief interview to reporters, all his communications with the outside world were deliberately cut off. Exactly one year later he spoke for the first time to his anxious relatives and friends from his underground prison. He remained down for another three months, then clambered to the surface, after an incredible feat of human endurance.

The Yugoslav speleologist had taken with him into his cave a number of domestic animals—cats, dogs, hens and ducks—who had adapted themselves remarkably well to the unfamiliar environment. The hens had continued to lay eggs, with little alteration in their normal pattern of behaviour, but the chicks had tended to remain close to the mother hens for a rather longer period than usual. Veljkovic observed afterwards that he had been miserably pestered by flies, indicating that insects could survive wet, cold and dark conditions provided they had enough food. In fact, they were spoiled in this respect, for the supplies of fresh fruit and vegetables that Veljkovic took with him rotted and became mouldy much sooner than expected.

The effects of prolonged solitude

Like the Frenchmen and others who had carried out similar tests previously, Veljkovic proved that it was possible for a man to live in a cold, dark and timeless environment for a prolonged period without seriously impairing his health. The many tests that he carried out while underground were of considerable value to scientists. He confirmed

These small figures of prehistoric animals were carved by Neolithic hunters and were found in the Vogelherd Cave in Germany. They represent a wild horse, a panther and a lion.

that after a few days away from daylight, and without a watch to guide him, man quickly loses all sense of time, and that his internal clock, which regulates all his normal bodily activities, works quite independently at its own pace. This inner clock controls his waking and sleeping, his heart beat and pulse rate, his breathing and blood temperature, the functions of his kidneys and his bowels. Veljkovic, like the two French cavers, also found himself resorting to a rapid sequence of waking and sleeping, and was firmly convinced that the minutes and hours were passing more rapidly than was in fact the case.

The findings of both sets of cavers were of great interest to scientists studying the problems of physical and mental behaviour in an entirely different environment—outer space. Although the absence of gravity poses far more complicated and serious problems, the illusion of timelessness is equally noticeable in space travel, with similar effects on the body and mind.

The lessons to be learned from such experiments do, however, have a more immediate application for cavers who, whether by accident or because of the nature of their expedition, are forced to spend any length of time below ground. A really extensive cave system, such as the 64-mile long Hölloch in Switzerland or the Flint Ridge system in Kentucky, now explored for almost 73 miles, involves large-scale explorations that may last for weeks on end. On such expeditions, regular bivouacs have to be set up, where some of the normal amenities of life above ground can be enjoyed —a roof, a warm sleeping bag and cooked food. As on mountaineering expeditions, it is sometimes possible for proper camps, with tents or bivouac cabins, to be left in perm-

anent positions, conveniently placed out of the wind and, where feasible, close to water. In any such lengthy operation, a complete day of rest is essential from time to time, partly for relaxation and partly to synchronize the work rhythms and patterns of the various members of the team.

Are we underground creatures?

To introduce the semblance of comfort and normality even in the muddiest and dampest conditions is of course of tremendous psychological importance. Nevertheless, it cannot be pretended that living in caves is a positive pleasure, even for the hardiest of individuals. A prolonged stay underground eventually dulls the mental activities. Concentration begins to wander and the sense of judgement is impaired. Ordinary actions take longer to perform and tempers start to fray. It becomes increasingly difficult to make meticulous observations or to take accurate measurements. These effects, of course, are neither sudden nor dramatic. A healthy, energetic man is not reduced in a matter of hours to a state of shambling helplessness. But the experienced caver, duly forewarned, will make a conscious effort to counteract such sensations, aware that his very survival may depend on alert faculties and split-second decisions.

Modern man is clearly not intended by nature to live below the earth's surface. But can we assume that our remote ancestors—the so-called cave men—were any better equipped for such an existence? Were they, in fact, cave men in the true sense of living permanently underground, or did they resort to caves as temporary shelters and hiding places? These are some of the questions that archaeologists

A bivouac in the Salzgraben Cave in Upper Bavaria.

A roof over one's head affords a sense of security as well as protection against dripping water and cold.

and palaeontologists have tried to answer, and if their recent investigations still leave many problems to be solved, they have at least succeeded in bridging some of the gaps separating us from our prehistoric relatives many thousands of years ago.

The earliest cave men

It was not until the 19th century that traditional theories of man's origin were seriously challenged by scientists, who sought to prove that human beings were only the latest link in a chain of evolution stretching back hundreds of millions of years. Since that time nobody has yet discovered the "missing link" between animals and humans, but any doubts as to the validity of the theory of evolution have been dispelled by the sensational finds of palaeontologists—the scientists who study fossil remains. Traces of long-extinct animals and men have been discovered in caves in different parts of the world, and although they have given rise to much controversy among the scientists themselves, it seems probable that the first humans on earth were living in caves more than two million years ago!

Dramatic cave finds during the latter half of the 19th century had convinced many, though by no means all, scientists that the rational and artistic creature known as man had a far longer history than had ever been suspected. Subsequent discoveries astounded even the most dedicated supporters of the evolutionary theory, for they pushed the dawn of human history back into a far more remote period.

In 1891 a skull cap and thigh bone were dug up in central Java. At first they were thought to have belonged to a giant ape, but close examination soon established that they were parts of the skeleton of an upright human being. He was given the name of *Pithecanthropus* ("ape-man"), thought to have lived during the early Ice Ages over 500,000 years previously. In 1927 about forty skeletons, belonging to another distinct type of hominid, were found in caves at Chou-Kou-Tien in China, not far from Peking. He was believed to have lived at about the same time as Java Man, or perhaps slightly later, and was given the name of *Sinanthropus*. The two types were subsequently pronounced to be so similar that they were given new specific names, *Pithecanthropus erectus* and *Pithecanthropus pekinensis*.

How old is man?

These and similar finds in the early 20th century were astounding enough, but a discovery of fossil remains at Taungs in Bechuanaland in 1924 had already suggested that man was older still. Later discoveries in the Transvaal seemed to confirm that *Australopithecus*, as this new specimen was named, was more than a million years old. The search was now centred on Africa. Fossil finds at the Olduvai Gorge in northern Tanzania were attributed to another ape-man called *Zinjanthropus*, who was proved to have used stone tools and tentatively dated as one and three-quarter million years old. A more recent find by Dr L. S. B. Leakey near the same site has unearthed another tool-using type called *Homo habilis,* said to be even older; and a discovery in Kenya in 1965 has been claimed to go back

Above right and centre: *these prints of bare feet were found embedded in the mud of a cave in northern Spain, and date from the Ice Age. Their owners probably made the cave a temporary shelter.*

Below: *these marks of hands, found in a cave in southern France, probably had magical significance. The Ice Age hunter may have sprayed pigment round the outlines of his own hands.*

Many caves contain human remains, though not all are as neatly arranged as these skulls of a man, woman and child.

two and a half million years.

Not all of these finds and dates have been universally accepted, but they have led to serious reassessment of the previously known facts about the origins of the human race. All these prehistoric ape-men clearly lived in protective caves and some used pieces of stone as weapons and tools, though there is no evidence of their having been shaped or fashioned. Little is known about how they lived, though reconstructions have been made of their probable appearance. Nor is much known of some of the alleged successors of these primitive humans—Heidelberg Man (so named after a finely preserved jaw bone found near Mauer in Germany), Swanscombe Man (after a skull fragment found in a gravel pit in Kent), or Rhodesian Man (a skull and other human remains in a cave at Broken Hill, Rhodesia). All these came to light comparatively recently and evidence is inconclusive. None of them is as significant as the find that was made in Germany in 1856, which lent such solid weight to the arguments of Charles Darwin and the supporters of his evolutionary theory and which was to spark off a controversy of unprecedented bitterness.

Neanderthal man

In the August of that year, some German quarry workers unearthed some bones from the small Feldhofer Cave, in a gorge above one of the tributaries of the Rhine, a few miles east of Düsseldorf. A local schoolmaster, Dr Fuhlrott, an expert on caves, pieced the remains together and declared them to be, not those of a cave bear, but of a recognizable prehistoric human being. The skull was high, with a low protruding forehead, and the indications were that it had housed a good-sized brain. Although English scientists agreed with the findings of Dr Fuhlrott, it was not until 24 years after his death that he was unanimously admitted to have been right. The individual to whom the bones belonged was given the name of Neanderthal Man, after the valley in which he had lived between 50,000 to 70,000 years previously.

Support for Fuhlrott's theory came in 1886 when similar bones, together with those of Ice Age mammals, were discovered below the entrance of a cave at Spy in Belgium. Linking these with earlier finds of human fossils—including one from the Steinbach cavern in Bavaria as far back as 1618—the scientists now declared that they all belonged to the amazingly advanced Neanderthal Man, who had lived as a hunter in southern and western Europe during the final period of the Ice Age.

In 1863 flint tools had been uncovered in the grotto of Le Moustier in France, and the discovery of another Neanderthal-type skeleton nearby in 1908 pointed unerringly to their owners. More light was thrown on the culture of these early hunters when, in the same year, the skeleton of a middle-aged man was found in the cave of La Chapelle-aux-Saints, not far from

Le Moustier. The body had been placed in a grave, surrounded by flint tools, stones and animal bones —clear evidence of a burial rite.

Proof that Neanderthal-type man had gradually spread eastwards through Europe, along the Mediterranean and North African coasts, and into Asia, was provided by discoveries of other skeletal remains in caves much farther afield. In 1950 the outlines of footprints were traced in the floor of the Grotta della Streghe in Italy. From their shape scientists deduced that they too had belonged to Neanderthal Man about 70,000 years before.

The first artists

The Neanderthal race apparently became extinct after surviving the final stages of the Ice Age and was replaced by a much more advanced and intelligent creature in the warmer period which followed. In 1868 a group of French railway workers came across a pile of bones, some of them animal but others clearly human, in a cave near Les Eyzies in the Dordogne. There were also stone tools and shell necklaces. Reconstruction of the skeletons indicated that Cro-Magnon Man, as he was subsequently named, was taller than Neanderthal Man, with a more upright stance and a larger brain, much more closely resembling *Homo sapiens*. Other finds suggested that he might have originated in Asia and moved westwards into Europe. In 1901 the remains of sixteen individuals were

The caves of northern Spain and southern France contain superb paintings from the Neolithic period. Above are engravings of a mare and foals in the Ebbro Cave; below is a flat painting of a bison from Altamira.

found in Italian caves. All but two were thought to have predated him. the others were more negroid and were thought to have predated him. They were given the collective name of the Grimaldi fossils.

These humans were evidently hunters and food gatherers, living in caves during the winter months, clothing themselves in animal skins,

and fashioning tools and weapons from bone and ivory. They probably lived about 30,000 to 40,000 years ago. But Cro-Magnon man had another claim to fame—he was the first known artist.

The painted caves

Man's first attempts to represent the objects that surrounded him and the animal and human figures with which he was familiar were crude and unpolished outlines, scratched with the fingers on the wet clay walls of the caves that sheltered him. Many such engravings have been traced in caves in northern Spain and southern France, and in some cases the imprints of the artists' feet and the marks of their hands on the walls have also been found. The

most ancient carving of a human figure is an eleven-inch ivory statue (reconstructed from 200 fragments) of a man, found in the Stadel Cave in Germany, which is claimed to be 32,000 years old. As time passed, man's artistic talent developed at an astonishing pace. Along with his weapons and domestic tools he fashioned tiny figures—many of them female—and traced geometrical patterns on stone and bone. His cave pictures began to take on recognizable forms and he began to daub them with colour. The extent of his abilities was revealed for the first time with the sensational discovery of the Altamira rock paintings almost a century ago.

During a fox hunt in 1868, a hound fell into a rock cleft and had to be rescued by its master. In so doing, he uncovered the entrance to a cave, but it was not until 1875 that the owner of the land, Don Marcelino de Sautuola, discovered animal bones and flint implements in the course of digging there. Encouraged by a Madrid geologist, Professor Juan Vilanova, Don Marcelino recommenced excavations in 1879. One day he took with him his small daughter Maria, who wandered down a passage and suddenly drew his attention to what appeared to be paintings. Don Marcelino flashed his torch over the roof and walls and excitedly confirmed her discovery. There, in black, violet and red, were the painted representations of bulls, wild boars, horses, deer and other creatures. Professor Vilanova then visited the cave and confirmed that the fossils already found were the remains of long-extinct animals—bison, deer, ibex and horse—precisely those whose images appeared so vividly on the cave walls and ceiling. He was convinced that the paintings dated from at least 30,000 B.C.

The doubters in disarray

Conventional scientists remained sceptical and neither Sautuola nor Vilanova lived to hear their theories confirmed. In 1895, two years after Vilanova's death, a prehistorian named Rivière found fossilized bone and horn objects, and wall engravings of animals, in the La Mouthe Cave in the Dordogne. They had been drawn some 270 feet

Head of a Stone Age precursor of a domestic cow, cut in bas-relief into a cave wall.

from the cave entrance, where it was pitch dark. A key to the way prehistoric artists worked and lived was given when a lamp was found in the same cave, itself adorned with the carving of an ibex.

The famous French prehistorian, Abbé Breuil, then discovered some tiny engravings—between two and twelve inches high—inside the entrance of the Combarelles Cave, also in the Dordogne. There were over 300 of them, including buffaloes, horses, stags, reindeer, mammoths, lions, bears and foxes. Even more exciting was the fact that there were also some likenesses of humans. Similar engravings were

light in Spain, especially in Santander province, the scope and scale of Altamira eclipses them all. The cave is 890 feet long and the chamber containing the majority of the paintings measures 60 feet by 30 feet and is between four and nine feet high. Most of the paintings are of bison in various positions, some standing still and others in motion, the irregularities and protuberances of the rock face being skilfully employed to lend them dimension and realism. Some of the colours are still unbelievably bright and the largest picture, of a hind, is seven and a half feet long. The other galleries contain engravings and

The Ice Age hunter believed he could ensnare his prey by representing it with soot and ochre on a cave wall. Here are two examples of his work. Left: *a highly stylized picture of a reindeer;* Right: *a scratch drawing on a cave wall.*

found in the cave of Font-de-Gaume. In 1902 Breuil visited Altamira and made copies of the paintings there. He was accompanied by a French scholar who had previously pronounced them to be forged and who now openly admitted his error. Breuil published his findings and the authenticity of the paintings in Altamira and other Spanish caves was established beyond doubt.

Although many other wonderful painted caves have since come to

paintings of more animals, about 150 in all. The absence of any human figures, both here and in most other Spanish caves, may be due to the animals' ritual significance—the belief that the paintings had magical powers which would enable hunters to trap them more readily. Animals were still regarded as natural enemies but were evidently treated with a measure of superstitious awe and respect, which found expression in art.

Lascaux

In the summer of 1940 a group of boys rescuing their dog from a crevice discovered a huge cavern near the Dordogne village of Montignac-sur-Vézère. It too contained spectacular paintings and soon became world-famous as the Lascaux Cave. The main hall at Lascaux measures 100 feet by 30 feet and is filled with wonderful action paintings of animals and humans. They are mostly outlined in black, some with dotted patterns, others washed with red or brown paint, the colours being even richer than those of Altamira. The animals too are more spirited, and there is one realistic scene of a bison wounded by a spear, attacking a hunter with a bird's head mask, who is keeling over backwards. Below the man is a figure of a bird, possibly representing the hunter's soul. Similar pictures, including the same spotted horses, have been found in the cave of Pech-Merle, thought to be even older than Altamira and Lascaux.

Cave art outside Europe

More than 120 caves, with comparable designs in the form of scratch drawings or paintings, have so far been located in Spain, France and Italy. But the painted caves of Europe are not unique. Recently, paintings of mammoths and cave bears were discovered in the Kapova Cave in the southern Urals, 450 feet from the entrance. And in scope and variety all are surpassed by the art of Africa, especially that of the Bushmen of Rhodesia, Southwest Africa and South Africa, with their lively representations of men and animals in black, white, brown, grey, yellow and red. Probably the style of the hunter-painter spread southwards via North Africa, but it was also carried as far north as Scandinavia and as far east as Siberia. A quite separate phenomenon is the cave art of the Australian aborigines, especially in Arnhem Land in the north. Here there is a living link with the past, for today's surviving aborigines still engrave and paint in a style very similar to that of their remote ancestors.

Temporary shelters

It seems likely that such caves were not regarded as permanent dwellings. Fossil remains show that prehistoric man settled with his family around the entrance to a cave, where there was a measure of natural light, and that once the winter or rainy season was over, he moved on, in true nomad fashion.

Below: *A map showing the distribution of painted caves in northern Spain and southern France.*

Bottom: *cave painting of a female red deer, six feet long, and small buffalo, from Altamira.*

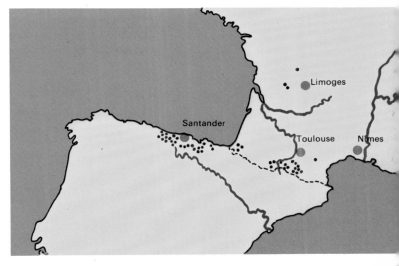

Flint tools such as this knife of the Upper Palaeolithic period have been found in many caves.

could get through. Centuries later, when the prehistorian arrived on the scene, he would find evidence of only the most recent occupation, but traces of earlier habitation might be revealed as he stripped away the successive layers. Eventually, clues would come to light, enabling him to date with amazing precision the various dates of occupation, sometimes separated by thousands of years.

Magic and religion

It is also evident that such caves were not only used for shelter. The fact that so many of the paintings and figurines have been found deep in the heart of some caves indicates that they must have held some magical or religious meaning, and that the art was not just intended to be a recreational exercise. In the huge Les Trois Frères, for example, there is a grotesque red and black painted figure, masked with an eagle's beak, owl's eyes, wolf's ears and stag's antlers, and dressed in an animal skin, with a horse's tail. It has been assumed that he is meant to depict some kind of wizard, for he is surrounded by pictures of all kinds of animals, including bears, horses, bison, lions and reindeer, engaged in different activities. They are seen making love, giving birth and in their death throes, one vivid painting showing a bear with blood streaming from its jaws. Experts believe that these pictures are replicas of the magical rites that once took place here.

Norbert Casteret also found marvellous rock drawings of animals in the Montespan Cave in the Pyrenees, as well as clay models of the same creatures. This too was probably a grotto where sacred rituals were once performed. In the Tuc d'Audoubert Cave, researchers

Thousands of years have passed since the Ice Age but hunters still use the Falkenstein Cave as a shelter.

As he learned how to use fire, he was able to introduce some warmth and light to the scene and probably retreated deeper into the cave. A prolonged stay, however, would have been uncomfortable due to the almost gale-force draughts sweeping through the cave and the choking effect of the smoke from his primitive lamp. If his hunting luck deserted him, he would be forced by pangs of hunger to move on in pursuit of the animals, leaving behind the remains of his meals, the ashes and charcoal of his fire, the bits and pieces of his tools and weapons.

Yet whatever these people left behind, no matter how sparse and fragmentary, provided the scientists with clues to the date of their occupation, however fleeting. Dust and dry leaves blowing into the cave might cover their remains, or they might be buried under rock breaking off the roof. Then a new group of tenants might move in and the entire process would be repeated. Gradually the space between the cave floor and roof would be reduced to a minimum and the entrance would become so narrow that only small burrowing animals have not only discovered the marks of bears on a clay slope but also signs of naked feet which stamped the soil in front of pictures of a male and female buffalo—further evidence of prehistoric man worshipping pagan spirits and gods.

Later habitation

The wonderful discoveries of painted caves and the fossil remains of Stone Age people rightly rank as the most important and exciting in prehistory. But caves also continued to serve as temporary shelters, homes, temples and burial places at later periods of man's development. Europe abounds in caves which were clearly occupied at one time or another. The Les Eyzies complex of grottoes in France bear traces of human occupation at intervals over a period of tens of thousands of years, cultural relics having been excavated from strata more than 30 feet deep. Similar caves exist throughout Germany and Austria, while in Britain too there are signs of Stone Age and Bronze Age occupations in caves from Lancashire and Derbyshire down to the Wye Valley and Devon. Some of these caves were clearly used even in Roman times, judging by pottery shards, coins

Ice Age sculptors cut and scraped animal figures out of ivory with their flint tools. This mammoth from the Vogelherd Cave is only two inches long.

Below and opposite page: *the oldest existing carving of a human figure was reconstructed from 200 ivory fragments.*

The exposed entrance to the Vogelherd Cave. Prior to its excavation, it was filled to roof level with debris.

and other conclusive evidence.

Outside Europe, the traces are more prolific. In the Middle East, for example, caves have been excavated on Mount Carmel and elsewhere, showing that they were used as shelters and sepulchres during the Stone Age and at later periods of history, as invaders and conquerors swept across the country from the the north and east, forcing the terrified inhabitants to seek refuge in the hills and mountains. In India there are some magnificently preserved cave temples, such as those at Ellora and on the island of Elephanta, outside Bombay, all dating from the 7th and 8th centuries A.D. In Egypt, among many splendid tombs and temples, mention must

be made of the rock-cut temples of Abu Simbel, dating from the reign of Rameses II, fourteen centuries before Christ, and now removed for safety to a new site high above the Nile. The physical transference of these immense and magnificent rock sculptures was a tremendous engineering feat.

In Russia, especially in the Crimea, there are fantastic caves, dating from prehistoric times, apparently serving as monasteries and catacombs. At Urgub in Anatolia, part of Turkey, there are ruins of an entire cave city, with homes, churches and chapels, some of them in extraordinary cone shapes, cut out of rock and still dotted about a broad plain.

Underground forts

Caves also sometimes served as natural fortresses. One celebrated example is the fortified cave of Lueg in Czechoslovakia (superseded by a 16th-century castle), which was reached by means of a rope ladder from the valley and which contained many emergency escape passages. Rain dripping from the cave roof provided an adequate supply of drinking water. It is likely that a similar function was served by the remarkable cliff dwellings once occupied by prehistoric Indian tribes in the southwestern part of the United States. The most spectacular of these is in Colorado's Mesa Verde National Park. In this huge Cliff Palace, more than 200 separate rooms and ceremonial chambers can be clearly identified. There are similar Indian cliff dwellings at Gila in New Mexico.

It might seem obvious that man, once he felt sufficiently confident of his skills and his ability to survive in a hostile natural environment, should ultimately emerge from his caves to build his permanent homes, villages and towns. Yet we have seen that even during historic times he has chosen, at times of special stress, to creep back into the caves for protection and security. In periods of war, for example, vital supplies of food and dumps of ammunition have been concealed in dry caves, safe from discovery and attack by land or air. Such caves also afforded protection for local residents in areas threatened by invasion, subjected to aerial bombardment or even overrun by an enemy. More surprising is the fact that even in the 20th century, there remain interesting examples of true troglodytes or cave dwellers, and not only confined to primitive communities.

Modern cave dwellers

In China, under the pressures of over-population and a local shortage of timber, cave cities have been built in the present century, one of

them at Yen, in the northern province of Shan-si. In Spain, similar problems, as well as the devastation caused by civil war, led to the use of natural caves, at first temporarily, then permanently. Especially impressive are the inhabited caves of Sierra de Guadix. Here literally is an underground city, whose inhabitants are renowned for their handicrafts. Their cave homes, some of them lit by electricity, are confortably cool in summer. There is no traffic, apart from mule carts, and all the communal buildings—school, church, taverns and cinema—are hewn from the rocks. It is a curious and rather refreshing phenomenon in a world too much obsessed with noise and bustle and machinery, especially since it has been undertaken from choice and not necessity. The residents of Sierra

The present castle of Lueg was constructed at the entrance to a cave, itself formerly used as a fortress.

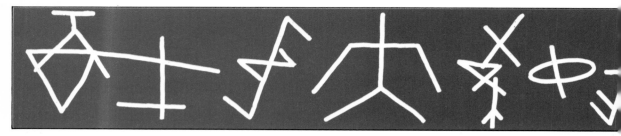

de Guadix appear as cheerful and as healthy as any of their neighbours who prefer living in more conventional surroundings. Clearly they are perfectly content with a pattern of life which must seem to offer them positive advantages.

It would be misleading, however, to deduce from this and other private and communal experiments in underground living that man is naturally adapted to cave life. He has little in common with those strange creatures described in the

The entrances to the artificial cave towns of the Anatolian highlands are sealed by great circular stones, often pierced with a central hole for defensive purposes.

next chapter, who have succeeded in acclimatizing themselves to a cave environment only by sacrificing certain vital processes. It is true that with the assistance of modern science and technology man has proved that he is capable of surviving for remarkably long periods in highly uncongenial surroundings. But the truth is that he has never been a natural cave dweller. There is, after all, a world of difference between survival and life!

These mysterious symbols were scratched on a cave wall in medieval times. Human figures and houses can be deciphered, others are unexplained.

Numerous cave dwellings have been found in these towers of volcanic tuff near Kayseri in Turkey. They are in remarkably good condition.

CHAPTER 3

CAVE ANIMALS AND PLANTS

Underground monsters

If monsters did not exist it would have been necessary for men to invent them—to paraphrase a famous French philosopher. Fire-breathing dragons, hellhounds with blazing eyes and blood-curdling roars, birds of prey in the service of the devil—it is all too easy to scoff at such creatures as the mere products of simple folk's superstitious fears and sick imagination. Yet have we ourselves the right, in an age of serious scientific examination into the identities of the Loch Ness Monster and the Abominable Snowman, to dismiss such beliefs out of hand as pure legend or fiction?

Primitive shepherds and hunters, seeing a trail of mist or current of warm air rising from an opening in a rock, or listening to the roar of a cave stream cascading into the open after a winter thaw, were quite convinced that such phenomena were directly caused by fiendish monsters trumpeting angry warning from their deep underground lairs. Nor has the passage of time necessarily brought enlightenment. Where myth and folk lore hold sway from the cradle to the grave, dull science is powerless to alter beliefs that have been cherished for generations.

Even today, many rational people nurse an uneasy feeling that a supernatural creature such as the Tazzel-wurm, an enormous dragon whose home is said to be in impenetrable Alpine caves, may turn out to be real after all.

Superstition and science

For such people, the discovery by cave explorers of piles of huge bones and skulls, merely serve to underline the probable truth of all these legends. Surely those colossal teeth and gigantic tusks could never belong to any animal known to living man. And who but fierce dragons could have destroyed such terrible creatures in their turn, picking them clean and leaving evidence of their meal in a neat heap of bones? The discovery of the occasional human skeleton only makes the whole affair even more sinister.

Nowadays, of course, we have the comforting assurances from the scientists that all these things have perfectly natural explanations, fitting tidily into an ordered historical scheme. There is no bellowing dragon in the bowels of the earth. In fact, it is the cave itself that is the bellower, as the level of a subterranean stream or river slowly rises

The only phosphorescent cave animals are the glow-worms of the Waitomo Grotto in New Zealand.

after a storm or thaw and forces trapped air noisily out of the cave entrance. As for the buried animal bones, these too have been scientifically explained, as belonging to no supernatural monsters but to creatures long extinct—cave bears, hyaenas, bison and the like.

The cave bear

Fossil remains of the huge cave bear have been discovered in their thousands all over Europe, includ-

This skeleton of a cave bear was reconstructed on a site in the Bärenhöhle where bear bones are still embedded in the floor.

ing Britain. One famous cave in the Swabian Alps of Germany was found to contain so many skulls and skeletons that it was immediately named the Bärenhöhle, or Bear's Cave. Bones of the animal are still embedded in the cave floor. The finds date only from 1949 and the cave itself consists of seven large chambers. In addition to the re-remains of the bears, speleologists found one enormous pile of human skeletons, probably victims of a

plague, as well as a charcoal-filled hearth and the bones of several kinds of domestic animal.

In other caves, the distinct marks of the bears' paws and claws have been detected on floors and walls, and in one case traces of the animal's fur in once-soft clay. The Dragon's Cave in Styria (Austria) yielded a colossal number of cave bears' skeletons—about 50,000. The cave had obviously once been a favourite hiding place and had been used by successive generations of animals for thousands of years. The accumulated bones and dung of the cave loam contained such a high percentage of phosphates that it was all carted away after the first World War by sixty goods trains, to be used as fertilizer.

Prehistoric paintings of the cave bear are surprisingly rare, but pictures in certain caves in southern France confirm the fossil reconstructions and indicate that the creature was about ten feet long and five feet high at the shoulder, about one and a half times as large as the modern brown bear (still found in parts of Europe) and even bigger than the grizzly bear. To prehistoric man, with his simple makeshift weapons, it must have been a formidable enemy, yet examination of its teeth suggest that it was better adapted for chewing vegetable matter than for ripping apart meat.

The bear cults

Only man himself and the powerful cave lion could claim to be a match for the cave bear. Possibly it sought refuge from them among the rocks, but more probably it entered to find shelter and to hibernate. The discovery of skeletons of young bears indicates that certain caverns were the sole preserves of the females, who sought them out when they were ready to give birth. Other skulls show conclusive signs of bone disease and other ailments, doubtless belonging to solitary old animals, who retired to such caves to die.

A cave in the St Gallen Alps of Switzerland revealed a stone container with seven bear skulls, all the snouts neatly facing the cave entrance. This suggests that the Stone Age hunters regarded the cave bear as a religious symbol and that on this occasion they had given the animals a ceremonial burial. Similar finds elsewhere indicate the existence of a bear cult, though some prehistorians believe that it was a creature to be feared rather than worshipped. It is interesting to note that among certain Siberian peasants and the primitive Ainu tribe of northern Japan, the bear is still hunted and revered. The Ainus keep the animals in captivity and then ritually sacrifice them, in the belief that they are thus releasing the divine spirits from their earthly guise.

Nobody knows exactly how or when the great cave bear became extinct. Man himself, with his inadequate weapons, could hardly have accomplished it on his own. Some experts have suggested that the Ice Age hunters may have kept the bears as prisoners, rather as the Patagonian Indians of southern Chile once imprisoned the giant sloth, but given the large numbers of animals, over-protection alone seems an implausible reason for their total disappearance. A more likely explanation is that the harsh climate and damp environment of the caves may have brought about the gradual physical decay of the animals' bones and organs, and that disease and death took their natural toll. Collections of bones showing signs of tumours and other crippling

Cave bears were larger than our modern species. They became extinct at the end of the Ice Age.

malformations supply supporting evidence for this theory.

Mammoths and hyaenas

The bear was certainly the best adapted of all the large prehistoric mammals for lengthy cave habitation, but fossil remains of many other creatures have also been excavated. The mammoth, for example, an ancestor of the modern elephant, was widely distributed throughout Asia, Europe and America. The woolly mammoth is the species most frequently depicted in cave drawings and paintings, and its remains have been found in Siberia and other Arctic regions, sometimes perfectly preserved after many thousands of years in frozen ground. This creature was apparently covered all over with thick, shaggy hair, and had a pair of large, curving tusks. Surprisingly, however, it must have been somewhat smaller than today's Asiatic elephant.

The bones and teeth of mammoths have been found in European caves, including many in England, Wales and Ireland, proving that herds of these hairy creatures once

The coat of arms of Hürben in Germany is a cave bear beneath a stag's antlers.

roamed freely over the hills and valleys now frequented by animals no larger or fiercer than the domestic cow or horse. There are numerous mammoth remains in the Mendips and other parts of southern England, but none of these provide evidence of the animal having been a real cave dweller. The same holds true of the Ice Age bison, frequently the subject of cave art but very rarely found in fossil form. Bison, reindeer, wild horses and smaller animals were all hunted by prehistoric man, and the discovery of piles of bones in caves indicates that they were part of the hunters' regular diet or that they were killed and dragged into the caves by larger wild animals.

One other animal, however, that can be ranked with the cave bear as at least a temporary cave dweller was the hyaena. This creature does not appear very often in cave paintings and was probably as unpopular with man and beast in those days as it is now, its role being a scavenger rather than a hunter. Fossil remains have also been found in southern England. The Hyaena Den, near the Wookey Hole, was found to

The dormouse is a typical troglophile, a frequent but not permanent resident of caves.

contain bones of these animals, as well as those of mammoths, rhinoceroses, wolves, bison, reindeer and other creatures. It is clear that it must have been similar in size and shape to the modern hyaena, that it had teeth powerful enough to crack the largest bones and that it retired deep into caves to devour its prey.

Cave dwellers and visitors

At some time—and for various reasons—all these wild and semi-wild animals became extinct. As the glaciers receded and the climate became warmer, their descendants emerged from the caves and adapted themselves to life in the woods, forests and steppes. Some survived in different forms, with changed physical characteristics and habits, others vanished completely. A few found the cave environment sufficiently congenial to settle underground permanently.

When we come to modern times, we find relatively few animals that may be classified as *troglobites*, or true cave dwellers, but quite a variety of small creatures which are described as *troglophiles*—animals who may be found living both in and outside caves. The species itself may exist in either location, but individual specimens are confined to one or the other. Some confusion tends to arise in the case of creatures such as earthworms and salamanders, found in the entrance or so-called threshold zone of caves.

In a third category are the *trogloxenes*—bears, bats, moths, etc.—who are temporary cave residents, seeking out such a habitat from choice, as for protection. Unlike troglophiles, they never complete their entire life cycle in caves. The dividing line between these last two categories is sometimes difficult to determine.

Many species of bats hibernate in caves, including the European mouse-eared bat. It is a harmless creature, unlike its vampire relative.

Bats

Among the troglophiles, creatures neither specially adapted for cave life nor entirely dependent on cave conditions, the most familiar and fascinating are the various species of bats. Although they occupy some caves in large colonies, bats regularly venture out at night to hunt. The longest cave in the world, the Carlsbad Cavern in New Mexico, was, as previously mentioned, discovered accidentally when a cowboy spotted tens of thousands of bats flittering and spiralling in the evening air in their quest for food.

Bats have long been the subject of story and legend and have acquired a rather fearsome and, on the whole, undeserved reputation as bloodsucking vampires. It is true that there are some species of Mexican cave-dwelling bats which do suck the blood of cattle and horses, and, as disease carriers, are emphatically more dangerous than others. But most of the ordinary bats of Europe and North America are by comparison quite innocuous,

feeding only on fruit or insects. They include the lesser and greater horseshoe bats, the long-eared bat, Daubenton's and Natterer's bats, the whiskered bat (all of these being common to British caves), the barbastelle and mouse-eared bats, and the free-tailed bat (the type found in the Carlsbad Caverns).

Bats are the only mammals with wings and their bodies are normally furry, with a fine covering of hair.

Colonies of closely packed bats hang from the cave roof during the winter.

A hooked protuberance on the edge of the wing enables them to move clumsily over the surfaces of cave walls, and the short legs, with their tiny claws, make it possible for them to suspend themselves upside-down from the cave roofs, either singly or in colonies. Unlike most mammals, bats do not possess a constant body temperature. In winter their heartbeat and breathing rates slow down, the body temperature drops to that of the cave

keeping records of sightings, scientists have been able to follow their migratory habits, as they do with birds. The lesser horseshoe bat does not venture far afield, sticking to the immediate neighbourhood of its cave all year round. Other species are more adventurous. In North America, the mouse-eared bats from the caves of Vermont, for example, flock in summer up to the Canadian border and southward and eastward to the Atlantic coast. In one of

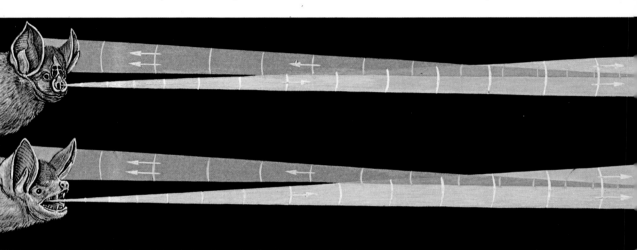

Bats have their own location-finding devices, varying slightly according to species. Horseshoe bats emit a directional band of sound through the nostrils, while vespertilionid bats, common to many temperate latitudes, transmit ultra-sonic impulses through the mouth. All use their ears to orientate themselves by means of the resultant echoes.

environment, and the bats hibernate. Some, such as the mouse-eared species, have a built-in regulating mechanism which wakes them up if and when the temperature of the cave drops to freezing point, in which case they simply fly deeper into the cave. Other species can survive with blood temperatures below freezing point.

After the hibernation season the colonies of bats often flock out on long journeys of several hundred miles to seek their summer quarters, returning to their original caves in the autumn. By ringing the bats, and

many experiments, a group of bats was transported about 500 miles from the cave site and released. All but a handful had found their way back to the original cave within three days. Other migrating bats have been observed as far as 800 miles from their point of departure. Similar observations have been made in Europe. A dwarf pipistrelle bat was recorded as having flown from a cave in the Ukraine to another in southern Bulgaria, a distance of more than 700 miles. Its rate of travel was leisurely, the journey taking ten weeks.

Vibrations and echoes

One of the most puzzling and interesting features of bat behaviour is their natural ability to move about without any difficulty in the dark. Some of the earliest investigators into the mystery had to resort to pretty barbarous methods in order to satisfy themselves that neither sight, taste, smell nor touch were in any way responsible. Nor was hearing in itself the answer, though

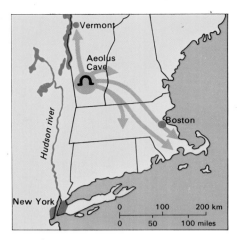

Bats leave their caves in spring for their summer quarters. The American mouse-eared bat flies from the Aeolus Cave in Vermont to the Atlantic coast near Boston.

can virtually fly from memory, giving out only a few precautionary pilot sounds.

Now that the individual seasonal movements of bats can be accurately recorded, it is also possible to gauge their various life spans. Some species have been found to live up to 25 years.

Although bats are not threatened with extinction, their numbers are liable to be greatly reduced by hordes of winter visitors who may, without

A lattice placed over a cave entrance affords protection to bats during hibernation.

The salanganes of North Borneo lay their eggs and breed in cave entrances.

some suggested that it was due to a kind of sixth sense, perhaps situated in the ears. More recent research has shown that the bat gives out ultra-sonic vibrations, which are emitted by means of a mechanism in the larynx. The frequencies of these signals vary according to species, and the sounds—detectable to the human ear only with the aid of special microphones—generate echoes that enable the bats to build up a precise sound picture of their immediate surroundings. This form of ultra-sonic orientation guides them unerringly to their nocturnal prey and enables them to flit about the interiors of the darkest caves without apparent difficulty. Where they are on familiar territory they

two eggs and then prepares a fresh nest for the following mating season. There are two good reasons for this foresight. The old nests tend to rot quickly and are collected by local inhabitants, then sold and exported to China to be made into the highly esteemed concoction known as "bird's nest soup". This has been a lucrative form of trade for centuries, and although attempts have apparently been made to supplement supplies by artificial methods, the natural nests are said to have unrivalled digestive properties!

The oil bird

Another night-flying cave visitor, also capable of "seeing" in the dark, is the guacharo or oil bird, a resident of caves in the Guacharo valley of Venezuela (now part of a national park) as well as certain caves in Trinidad. This strange bird was first discovered by the German naturalist Alexander von Humboldt, at the beginning of the 18th century. It is about the size of a domestic hen, with a wingspan of three and a half feet, has a vulture-like beak and gives out a shrill cry somewhat like that of a nightjar. The oil bird comes

Salanganes' nests are collected to make bird's nest soup.

knowing, disturb their hibernation patterns. The only sensible solution is for authorities to cover cave entrances with a lattice during the winter, through which the bats can fly in and out as necessary.

The salangane

There are certain kinds of cave-dwelling birds which also seem to possess a similar kind of inbuilt location finder. One such is the extraordinary salangane, a relative of the swallow. Although there are more than a dozen species, only three of them are regular cave dwellers, confined to Borneo and other Indonesian islands. The salangane constructs its nest close to the cave entrance by means of a glutinous spittle, secreted under the tongue, which flows freely at mating time. The bird builds the nest patiently over a period of several weeks, lays

Right and far right: cocoons of cave spiders hang like lanterns from the roof.

out of its cave only at night in search of food, mainly in the form of seeds and nuts. Its common name is derived from the layer of fat from the abdomen, which exudes a clear fluid, used for centuries past by local Indians as oil for cooking and lighting purposes.

Other kinds of birds, such as owls and condors, often make their nests in small caves and on cliffs near to cave entrances, but these cannot properly be classified as true cave dwellers or visitors; nor can the many animals, such as dormice, who hoard nuts in caves, or badgers and foxes, who often dig burrows among debris collected around the entrance to caves.

Without sight and colour

So much for the temporary cave dwellers. We come now to the troglobites proper, the cave creatures who live in a world of perpetual darkness. Among them are numerous species of fishes, crustaceans and insects, many of them completely colourless and sightless, but compensating for the absence of eyes by having exceptionally acute senses of hearing, smell and touch.

The guacharo or oil bird lives in caves in northern Venezuela and Trinidad. Its bright plumage shows up clearly in the gloomy surroundings.

These curious creatures display physical characteristics and behaviour patterns very different to those of closely related species above ground, indicating that over the course of many centuries they have somehow adapted themselves to the special conditions of subterranean life. Such characteristics as lack of pigmentation and degeneration of eyes (and, in the case of certain insects, of wings) may be caused by insufficient thyroid hormone secretion. Other experiments suggest that diminished oxygen consumption may also be a contributory cause. Growth tends to be irregular and erratic, some species being larger, others smaller than their terrestrial counterparts. Certain

The proteus or blind cave newt is probably the most primitive of cave animals, living in the karstic caves of Yugoslavia.

insects are unusually slender, with abnormally long appendages to compensate for absence of wings.

Whatever the reasons for these distortions, each species has managed to adapt itself to the dark, humid, constant-temperature conditions of cave existence. Any sudden alteration in their environment is liable to be fatal. The unexpected introduction of light, whether natural or artificial, may lead to instantaneous death.

Some of these unusual and fascinating underground creatures merit special mention by reason of their individual appearance or behaviour. But even these are representative of only a very few of the innumerable species of tiny organisms that have thus far been identified and studied. Because of the special hazards and difficulties involved, research in this field is still in its early stages. Most of the work already done has necessarily been confined to caves situated in the temperate zones of Europe and North America. The discoveries that have been made are extremely interesting but comparatively little is known of tropical cave life.

Fishes and crustaceans

The few cave-dwelling fishes that have so far been located are all American. Two of them inhabit the Mammoth Cave and other caves in Kentucky. *Amblyopsis spelaus* grows to about five inches in length and has a large mouth. It is white and blind, with sensitive tactile organs distributed over its body and head. The fish is a live-bearer, related to the carps and pikes, and the family contains species which possess normal vision. Another species, *Typhlichthys subterraneus*, is also white, but takes on a faint tinge of colour if subjected to light. A very similar animal is the blind cave fish of Mexico, *Anoptichthys jordani*.

Underground crustaceans include many pool-dwelling shrimps or amphipods, the strangest of which is the blind cave shrimp, *Niphargus*. This too is an absolutely colourless creature and species of the genus are widespread throughout British caves. The shrimp swims in a sideways direction and its tactile sense is acutely developed, with the long feelers constantly in motion as it scoops up minute aquatic plant life from shallow pools. These small basins of water are teeming with animals as well, including microscopic water fleas, only a few millimetres in length. Some of these are amphibious, being capable of surviving equally well on the cave floor and walls. Of a similar minute size are the springtails, which breathe through their skins. They too are well suited to wet, humid conditions but lack the ability to jump free if they happen to land in a cave pool.

There are many kinds of aquatic and amphibious worms to be found in caves, living in ground water or mud. Some of these are also blind and colourless, others are so minute that they have defied all efforts of

scientists to catch and study them. One aquatic worm named *Prostoma* can live only in water of a certain temperature range. It is a voracious carnivore, equipped with a sting with which it ejects poison into the bodies of its victims.

Cave amphibians

Cave-dwelling amphibians are particularly fascinating. They all belong to the order Urodela, which includes the newts and salamanders. Such creatures normally breathe through their skins, and since these surfaces must be kept moist, the humid atmosphere of caves suits certain species admirably. Almost all the salamanders are North American animals and some of them, which possess normal sight, are found only close to cave entrances. The *Typhlotriton* is an intermediate case, for the larvae have normal eyes and proper pigmentation. After metamorphosis, however, they probe deep into the caves, losing both their colour and sight. By contrast, the *Typhlomolge* of Texas is a true cave-dwelling salamander, living exclusively in water and drawing breath through fringed gills. These, surprisingly, are vivid red, while the rest of the body is white. Another species of salamander is native to the Alps and western Balkan mountains.

The blind cave newt

A curious, salamander-type cave dweller, confined to Europe, is *Proteus anguinus*, variously known simply as the proteus or the blind cave newt. This remarkable creature, certainly many thousands of years old, is exhibited to visitors in the caves of Postojna, in the karst region of Yugoslavia. The animal has an eel-like body, about eight to twelve inches in length, a triangular head and a rudder-like tail. The proteus is not entirely colourless, its body having a pinky-white tinge. This is actually the blood glistening through the skin, which gives a rosy hue to the three pairs of external

Unlike the creatures of the ocean depths, cave animals—with the exception of the Waitomo glow-worm—are not luminous. Most of them lack colour completely.

gills. The colour is so reminiscent of that of human flesh that some people call it the "human fish". In addition to the gills, the animal also possesses tube-like lungs.

The female lays her eggs in the cold water of the cave or attaches

Like many other cave animals, the cave water flea is white and its eyes are almost completely atrophied.

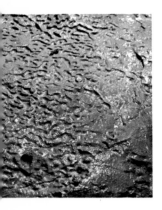

Above: *bacteria infest the cave mud. They play an important role in the subterranean food chain.*

Right: *spherical algae, unlike bacteria, thrive on light.*

Two species of hibernating cave moths.

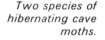

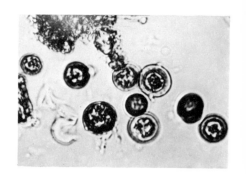

them to stalagmites. Experiments in aquaria have indicated, however, that the young may be bred successfully in water of a considerably higher temperature than is normal underground. In fact, it appears that when the water is below a certain temperature the cave newt will give birth to live young, whereas if it is higher the young will hatch from eggs—an extraordinary phenomenon.

When born, the baby proteus has tiny black pinpoints of eyes, covered by layers of skin, but as it develops, the eyes disappear completely, until it is quite blind. Another odd feature is that at birth the animal's colour is grey, with the lighter colour only developing slowly. If the creature is later exposed to continuous light, the dark pigmentation will return, until it becomes almost black.

The blind cave newt has two pairs of limbs, one placed forward near the head, the other at the rear of the body. One pair has three toes, the other two. The legs, however, are very weak and it is the disproportionately long tail which provides the main motive force. As with other blind cave animals, the senses of smell, hearing and touch are highly efficient.

Beetles, snails and spiders

The first of various species of cave beetles was also discovered in the Postojna Cave. It too proved to be completely blind, with sensitive hairs on the legs and antennae, and with wing covers but no wings. Other blind cave beetles display similar characteristics, and are either white or extremely pale in colour. They are usually carnivorous ground beetles, and since their respiratory organs and openings show degeneration, it is generally assumed that

they breathe through their skin.

The cave-dwelling fungus gnat also absorbs oxygen through its skin. It has an abnormally large head and the mucus secreted in its salivary gland forms grey spider-like threads, which enable the insect to travel across the surface of cave walls. Other strange species of gnats either lack wings or make no use of them in the cave darkness.

The various types of snail that have been found underground may not be true cave dwellers, but have probably either crawled in or been swept in by water. Unlike other subterranean creatures, far from losing their colour or having very pale pigmentation, they tend to become darker than comparable standard surface species.

In certain caves in southeast Asia, cave snakes have been reported. They are white in colour and feed on various bats.

Spiders are frequently found in caves, some at the entrance and others in the deepest recesses. *Meta menardi*, for example, is only an occasional visitor, spinning a cocoon-like nest, which is suspended from the cave roof by a thread. This species is preyed upon by other genuine cave-dwelling spiders, including blind, albino types.

These then are just a handful of the living creatures who make their homes underground. Among insects not separately mentioned, there are also many species of flies, bees, wasps, cockroaches, crickets, moths, mosquitoes and flies. Apparently unique to New Zealand are certain glow-worms—predatory larvae of flies— which illuminate the grotto of Waitomo. Other insects are caught by means of thin, spider-like threads, and visitors can see them in their thousands as tiny pinpoints of light all over the cave roof. No other kind of cave creature is known to possess light-emitting organs, similar to those developed by many deep sea fishes.

Adapting to cave life

Scientists are steadily increasing their knowledge about cave animals and the ways in which they live, but already it is evident that they differ enormously from species to species and according to where in the world their cave homes are situated.

By no means all of these creatures behave like the blind cave newt, which over the centuries has evolved into a less active and smaller version of its surface relatives. Nor are they all exclusively cold-loving species. The temperature of most caves is moderate and thus suitable for both warm- and cold-blooded creatures to live comfortably alongside one another. Many cave animals, such as beetles, fishes, snakes and grass-hoppers, have terrestrial counter-parts better suited to tropical climates, yet they too have managed to adapt themselves to the cooler environment of caves.

Many of these subterranean creatures are, however, more obviously cold-loving species. Such, for instance, are the various types of flat worms which, during the Ice Age, bred freely in the melted waters of glaciers, and whose descendants reside in the polar regions or in mountain caves. As the lower reaches

of the glaciers gradually became warmer, such worms retreated to the source regions or into subterranean water courses, where the temperature remained far colder.

Yet it must not be assumed that all the animals found today in caves necessarily found their way there of their own volition. A few of them were clearly suited at the outset to the most extreme of subterranean conditions, but others, forced to resort to such an environment, had to adapt themselves gradually. After many generations, their descendants were so tolerant of these conditions that they could endure no other form of environment.

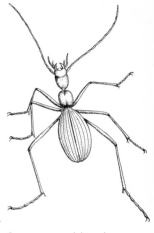

Cave ground beetle.

Survival of the fittest

The mystery of this continuous pattern of adaptation was answered in the 19th century by Charles Darwin and his colleagues, with the theory of evolution and the correlated doctrine of "survival of the fittest". The members of any single species are always slightly different from one another in physical make-up or behaviour. Some are bigger, stronger and more agile than others; less well equipped members of the species fail to survive harsh conditions, such as exceptionally low temperatures, to which the stronger members can successfully adjust. Certain physical changes in the evolutionary process are positive advantages in difficult environments, such as the improved sense of hearing and touch, perceptible in all true cave-dwelling creatures. Lack of colour can itself be beneficial, the skin being of thinner texture and more sensitive to touch.

Equally clearly, many animals found it impossible or increasingly difficult to adapt to cave conditions. Some became extinct, others abandoned the caves to seek more

Cave dung beetle.

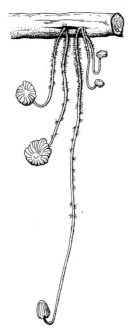

Fungi growing in the darkness of caves form very long stalks and tiny caps.

clement conditions outside. Those troglobites who did remain and who still survive have managed not only to accommodate themselves to the absence of light but have learned to exist on the relatively scarce sources of food available to them.

Subterranean plant life

Many cave animals have apparently been able to survive for tens of thousands of years with a minimum of food, some indeed without any proper form of nutrition whatsoever. The proteus or blind cave newt, for example, is able to do without food for as much as three years. Other creatures can feed exclusively on cave mud. Others find sustenance in the form of smaller cave animals, vegetable and animal debris, bat guano, leaves, seeds and grasses blown into the cave, and native cave plants.

Green plants as we know them cannot grow in the darkness of caves. Seeds blown or carried into a cave may begin to grow but will never develop properly. Such plants need chlorophyll for growth and survival and cannot thrive in fissures where no light penetrates. Only near the entrances of some caves, where there is a proper balance of light and moisture, do we sometimes find clusters of green ferns or certain kinds of dwarf flowering plants. Similarly, at the thresholds of some sea caves there is often an abundance of marine plant life.

Fungi and bacteria

The plant life of the interior of caves is usually comprised of fungi and bacteria, which do not require any light for survival and multiplication. Organic material quickly attracts fungi. Wooden beams and ladders, often set up in show caves, are rapidly penetrated by threads of fungi, flimsy constructions forming long stems with tiny caps. In certain tropical caves, one type of fungus causes a form of lung infection, fortunately with no long term effects.

Growths of bacteria are often found near cave entrances and are regularly carried by the wind into the interior, covering walls and the upper surfaces of stones and rocks with a slimy brownish coating. Bacteria also proliferate on animal bones and droppings. The spores of moulds, brought in by water, also settle as white growths on organic matter and decomposed wood.

Scientists came across an interesting phenomenon in the Aggtelek Cave in Hungary. Samples of a gleaming black encrustation, at first thought to be soot, were examined under the microscope and found to be composed of a rare iron-bacteria, capable, by chemical means, of converting inorganic material into organic life. These same iron-bacteria were also found to be present in some deposits taken from cave walls and floors, and would seem to provide added sustenance for certain cave-dwelling organisms. The discovery of such bacteria lends support to those scientists who believe that cave deposits such as moonmilk have also been caused by bacterial action.

Algae

The green scum sometimes seen floating in cave pools and the similar green stains marking cave walls are caused by tiny primitive organisms known as algae. These plants (though some scientists claim them to be animals) are remarkably prolific, with a multitude of aquatic (both freshwater and marine), aerial and terrestrial forms. These last types are capable of surviving for excessively long periods without any sustaining moisture, and can thrive both above and below ground. Some are especially addicted to limestone, both in rocks and water, and some, under microscopic examination, have proved to secrete lime themselves. In the sea, algae play a vital part in the food chain of fishes and other underwater creatures. It is certain that they fulfil a similar function in the subterranean world.

Most of the algae that flourish underground are of the blue-green type. It is remarkable that they should contain this cell pigmentation while growing in utter darkness. Nobody has yet explained how they grow under these conditions or what they feed on. Possibly there is some link between algae and bacteria which may in due course be discovered. Much remains to be done in the field of cave botany.

Let there be light

The introduction of artificial light into this black world, as in the great show caves, has startling and immediate effects on plant life underground. Layers of green vegetation appear from nowhere, much to the satisfaction of cave-dwelling insects such as the springtails. Jelly-like beds of blue algae, lawns of moss and clumps of miniature ferns begin to form on the stalactites and even cluster around the lamps themselves.

Although the effect of this burgeoning green life is often very beautiful, such artificially induced growths are not always welcome. In the painted caves of Lascaux, for example, the rapid spread of algae

When exposed to artificial lighting dripstone formations are often covered with green algae.

threatened the pictures on the roof and walls. Switching off the lights and restricting the flow of visitors proved to be the only solution in efforts to save the priceless paintings, which had been preserved only by reason of the complete darkness and lack of air movement for some 20,000 years. This was a serious decision for the French authorities to make, for the caves had naturally been an outstanding tourist attraction. Cautious experiments were made during 1969 to readmit a limited number of visitors, but they proved impracticable. Unfortunately, therefore, the Lascaux Caves are once more closed indefinitely to the public, and the most spectacular examples of French cave art are entombed as for centuries past. It is to be hoped that scientists may soon find a solution to this unforeseen problem, as it is only too likely to recur in caves elsewhere in the world.

This unexpected occurrence should perhaps serve as a small warning to man as he ventures into new and unexplored regions of the world below the earth's surface. It is a sad comment on human greed and thoughtlessness that wherever he has gone, whether in the interest of science or adventure, man has inadvertently interfered with nature's delicate balance. It is happening in deserts, mountains and jungles. It may even have happened on the moon. Inevitably, it must have its effect, however gradual, however superficial, on the living organisms below the ground. It may be a long time before the need arises to set up subterranean reserves or to appeal for funds to protect threatened forms of cave life, but speleologists should be aware of their responsibilities in this highly complex area of research, and tread warily.

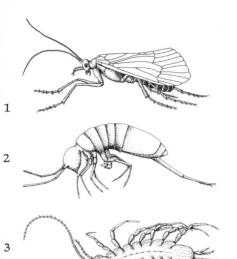

1

2

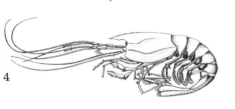

3

Right: *The growth rhythm of cave mosses depends on the artificial lighting to which they are exposed. In winter, when the lighting is switched on for very short periods, growth slows down or ceases. In summer the width of the leaves increases. Each growth section corresponds to a year.*

Opposite page: *Mosses and ferns develop as soon as lamps light up the cave gloom.*

4

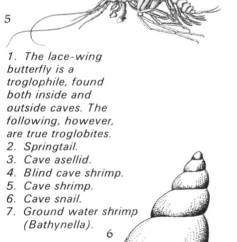

5

1. The lace-wing butterfly is a troglophile, found both inside and outside caves. The following, however, are true troglobites.
2. Springtail.
3. Cave asellid.
4. Blind cave shrimp.
5. Cave shrimp.
6. Cave snail.
7. Ground water shrimp (Bathynella).

6

7

Experiments are being conducted to get rid of unwanted light-induced flora by irradiating them with ultra-violet light.

Wissenschaftliche
Versuchsanla
des
Instituts für spezielle
der Universität Tübing.

Bitte nicht berühren (UV-Strahl.

CHAPTER 4

THE MAKING OF CAVES

Caves of lava

The broad definition of a cave is "a natural underground cavity", sometimes qualified by the phrase "large enough to permit human entrance". It may be distinguished from a pothole by the fact that it extends in a horizontal rather than vertical direction, and the term may be applied not only to a single cavity but to a connected group of caves, generally known as a cave system.

In considering the origin and structure of caves, speleologists classify them in different ways. The majority have been formed by gradual natural processes over millions of years, but a distinction is usually made between so-called primary and secondary caves. Primary caves are those that were formed at the same period as the rock which encloses them. Secondary caves, which are far more common, were formed at a later date by the breaking down or removal of rock material by external forces—rain water, ocean waves, winds and ice. In the first category are most lava caves and certain other specialized forms. In the second are the limestone caves, comprising the great majority of all caves. These terms, however, are not completely fool-proof and for present purposes

need only serve as a rough guide. It is more convenient to examine them in a more general way, looking in some detail at the way in which limestone caves are formed and glancing at others under the broad classifications of volcanic or lava caves, wave caves, wind caves and ice caves.

Volcanic caves were originally created by the flow of fiery lava, which in due course cooled and congealed. When a volcano erupts, the white-hot lava overflows the rim of the crater and courses slowly down the slope of the mountain in a viscous stream. As the surface of the molten lava cools, a crust is gradually formed. After a few hours it may already be thick and solid enough to walk upon. Inside this hardening shell, however, the liquid lava continues to bubble and flow, as if it were enclosed within a huge pipe, cutting out a long tunnel. Portions of the still-soft roof may collapse from time to time into the tunnel, causing blocks and cavities. In such a way, immense smooth-walled caverns with vaulted roofs and stalactite-type formations may be moulded out of the natural lava flow.

An American geological survey team recently set out to investigate the crater of Kilauea Iki on the

Left: *the raging torrent has cut deep tunnels through the mountain rocks. A passage in the Dachsteinmammut-höhle (Mammoth Cave) in Upper Austria.*

Convulsions of the earth's crust broke the surface of old flows of lava and formed caves with warm-water pools, as in northern Iceland.

island of Hawaii, which had erupted a short while before. The fiery lake of lava had hardened sufficiently to form a reddish-brown crust and the team set up its drilling equipment in the centre of the crater itself. After drilling through eighteen feet of solid basalt, the drill suddenly plunged into a hollow. Twelve feet farther down it hit a layer of porridge-like lava, recording a temperature of 1,150°C. Between the molten lava and the crust on the crater floor, a cave had been formed, the crust acting as a lid. This was admittedly a somewhat unusual cave formation, with little guarantee that it would last, but it was nevertheless an interesting example of the way in which some primary caves can come into being.

Not far from the volcano of Kilauea Iki, visitors can be guided round a lava cave of more ancient origin. The cool, moist chamber measures over 300 feet in length and there are ferns growing at the entrance. On the opposite side of the world, on the island of Lanzarote, in the Canaries, there is a volcanic cave which can claim to be the largest on earth. It is more than three and a half miles long and is a colossal 690 feet high. At one time it was large enough to conceal the entire island population from slave traders. Today it is a tourist attraction, complete with air-conditioned restaurant and with a hole in the roof, formed by the original flow of lava, which provides the cave with a natural shaft of light.

On Mount Etna, the still active volcano on the east coast of Sicily, which has erupted more than a hundred times in the past 2,000 years, there are innumerable lava caves near the summit, where snow gathers in winter, and round the subsidiary cones that have sprung up along the rock fissures. In

This huge cave was formed under the solidified lava lake of Kilauea Iki in Hawaii. In the background is the smoking crater of Halemaumau.

classical times huge blocks of ice were cut from the caves' interiors and transported on the backs of mules down to the foot of the mountain. There the ice was mixed with fruit juice and sugar to make what was probably the world's first ice cream!

In places where a flow of lava passes over a marsh or shallow lake, the underlying body of water may boil to form huge bubbles and arches, which often explode like miniature volcanoes. On the shores of Lake Myvatn, in northern Iceland, dozens of such volcano-like protuberances stud the bleak landscape. Some of them are large enough for a person to climb down inside. In the same region visitors can enter the famous lava caves of Storagja and Grojotagja. These are aligned along a huge crack from which volcanically heated water rises, enabling visitors to enjoy a warm bathe even in winter.

Left: caves have been formed on volcanic islands as molten lava flows away under a solidified lava stream. This picture is of Stromboli.

67

Waterfalls and waves

By far the largest number of caves are formed from limestone, a sedimentary rock built up by primitive marine plants and animals in the seas hundreds of millions of years ago. This soft rock, consisting chiefly of calcium carbonate, is part of the earth's crust and is deposited in layers of varying depths throughout the world. In places it may extend down only a few feet; elsewhere, especially in central and western Europe, limestone potholes may be thousands of feet in depth.

We shall shortly be examining some of the ways in which limestone caves and potholes are formed, but

Hollows are formed behind the advancing calcareous tuff edge of the waterfall. (Plitvice).

first we must glance at a specialized type of primary limestone cave, formed from calcareous tufa or tuff. Layers of lime are often deposited in stream or river beds and are moulded by the running water into bar-like shapes. These attract growths of freshwater algae which, as the water becomes warmer, entrap the tiny lime crystals and are in turn enclosed by encrustations of lime. In the course of time other forms of vegetable and animal matter, including mosses, grass, leaves, snail shells and driftwood, washed down by the current, become embedded and petrified inside the growing bars of lime. Eventually, the growths of lime are large enough to encrust and petrify shrubs, bushes and small trees at the water's edge, so that a natural dam is built up across the stream or river. The rock of which this dam is made is light and porous, containing many small hollows, and is known as tufa or tuff.

Sometimes the hollows in the rock are large enough to form real caves, especially on the steep front edge of such a barrier, over which a waterfall is pouring. The spray of the waterfall then encourages the growth of pillows of moss where more lime accumulates. Gradually, the projecting growths of moss and algae are petrified by the deposits of lime and break off under the weight. The fragments lying at the foot of the barrier may then form a wall which attracts additional moss and algae growth, and so the process continues. Ultimately, the petrified wall will rise high enough to enclose the hollow behind the waterfall.

Such caves of calcareous tuff are usually very irregular in shape. Yet even though a stream or river may be running directly over them, they are often surprisingly dry and airy. The thick growths of moss and algae

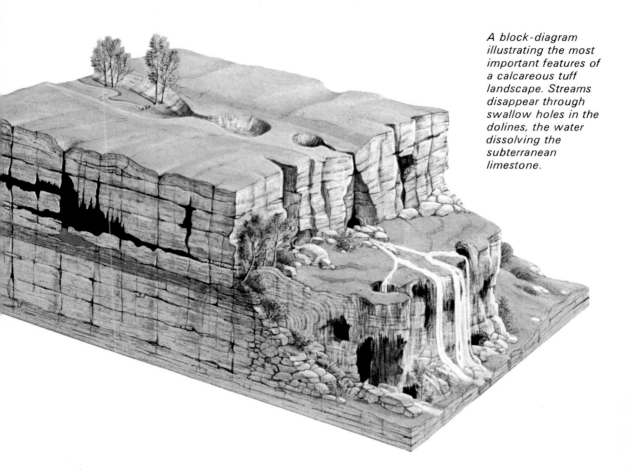

A block-diagram illustrating the most important features of a calcareous tuff landscape. Streams disappear through swallow holes in the dolines, the water dissolving the subterranean limestone.

seal every crack in the river bed.

On the southern coast of Turkey, near the town of Antalya, a river drops as a broad waterfall over a series of fine calcareous tufa caves. But the most famous examples are the caves of the Plitvice Lakes on the Croatian plateau, in Yugoslavia. Here, in a river valley five miles in length, lie more than twenty lakes and as many caves, formed behind barriers of calcareous tuff. The highest of the lakes is about 2,000 feet above sea level and cascades of crystal-clear, lime-rich water plunge from one level to another, dropping 465 feet in the process. The lakes and their caves are deservedly among the most spectacular tourist centres in Yugoslavia.

Thick blocks of calcareous tuff may also develop on mountain sides, immediately beneath springs of lime-bearing water. In time, barriers of tufa, waterfalls and primary caves are formed, similar in structure to those encountered nearer sea level.

Plants in calcareous water are completely encrusted with lime, algae playing a vital role in the process. (Plitvice).

Other types of caves may be cut by waves in the open sea or along sea coasts. One of the most famous of these is Fingal's Cave, on the island of Staffa in the Inner Hebrides, commemorated in music by the composer Felix Mendelssohn. The rock itself is hard basalt of volcanic origin, and the cave was formed by the continuous battering of the waves against the base of the immense hexagonal pillars that now line the walls.

In a wave-cut cave, huge fragments of rock are continually hurled against the walls so that the hollow gradually increases in size. Eventually, the unsupported roof collapses, so that only the entrance portal is left standing.

Some spectacular caves are found in tropical waters in the vicinity of coral reefs. Hollows are formed between the blocks of coral and in time these are bridged over and enclosed. Such beautiful underwater formations are normally only accessible to deep sea divers, but from time to time a hollowed reef may be lifted above the surface by

Left: the famous Plitvice lakes and waterfalls were formed when the river built up barriers of calcareous tuff across the valley.

Calcareous tuff and the concretionary limestone known as travertine have been used for building since ancient times. Left: *St Amandus Church, Urach, built of sandstone and calcareous tuff.* Right: *the ancient baths of Hierapolis in western Turkey, built of travertine.*

A beach cave in Monte Gargano, the spur on the Italian "heel".

an earthquake or volcanic disturbance. In such cases it is virtually impossible to determine whether it is a natural coral formation or whether it is really a secondary cave, formed by wave action.

On a steep stretch of coastline which is liberally laced with caves or vertical cracks, continuous pressure of waves may lead to the for-

mation of blowholes some distance inland, through which the water will burst like a fountain or geyser. Celebrated examples of these can be seen in Sardinia and Hawaii.

Limestone caves

Examples of lava, calcareous tuff, reef and wave-cut caves are com-

A block-diagram showing the main types of caves along steep coasts, including blowholes, natural arches and various kinds of wind-formed caves.

The southern cape of Iceland has a natural arch.

paratively rare. Most of the caves explored and studied by speleologists—including nearly all the famous show caves of both the Old and New Worlds—are secondary caves which have been formed by the continuous action of water on limestone rock.

These caves are sometimes called karstic caves, though the term *karst*

is more specifically applied to the mountainous region around Trieste, on either side of the border between Italy and Yugoslavia. This area contains extensive outcrops of limestone, which soak up rain water very rapidly, and is characterized by enormous caves and broad underground rivers.

Limestone is a sedimentary rock,

Above left: "Spouting Horn" is the name of this blowhole on the north coast of the island of Oahu.

Above: *The entrance of this wave-cut cave is cut off by the flood tide.* Below: *the ebb tide reveals an entrance large enough for a boat to enter.*

This wave-cut cave on the Bay of Antalya is large enough to admit a cutter.

of organic origin (unlike igneous rocks such as basalt and granite), which was laid down in the sea as sediment several thousands of millions of years ago. The large limestone caves of Europe and America, situated in hill and mountain regions, have probably been formed during the last 300 million years, at a time prior to the appearance on earth of the great dinosaurs.

Limestone rock contains different layers, known as bedding planes, which are separated by horizontal breaks or stratification lines. The bedding planes—then as now—were normally horizontal in direction, but the pattern tended to be irregular, frequently sloping in so-called dips and folds, or containing natural faults, which broke the continuity of the different strata or layers. These kinds of deformities were generally caused by violent movements of the earth's crust, including volcanic eruption, and

such disturbances also raised the limestone deposits well above sea level.

Under the steady, persistent increase of these natural pressures, further vertical cracking took place, leading to ever greater disruption of the neat horizontal pattern. These new fissures, at right angles to the bedding plane—known to geologists as joints—either affected a single bed or struck down in a jagged network through several layers, in which form they are called master joints. The scene was now set for water to seep through the joints and initiate the natural processes resulting in the formation of the limestone caves.

Corrosion and corrasion

Water does not, in the normal way, soak through limestone rock, but simply lies on the surface. But once it had found its path into the

The roof of this limestone cave has collapsed, leaving only an arch standing.

rock, either along the break lines of the bedding layers or down through the joints, the water began to dissolve the limestone. Over a period of many thousands of years the water infiltrated deeper and deeper, following the maze of cracks and the natural slopes; and the dissolution process was speeded up by the fact that it was rain water at work. This particular example of erosion, the dissolving of rock giving steady enlargement of natural fissures, is known as corrosion.

Certain types of rock, such as gypsum, are capable of being dissolved over a period of time by pure water. This is not the case with limestone rock, which consists in the main of calcium carbonate, in the form of calcite. Limestone, though hardly affected at all by pure water, is, however, soluble in dilute acid. Rain water, as it falls through the atmosphere, absorbs minute quantities of carbon dioxide from the air. As it soaks into the soil it collects more carbon dioxide from bacteria and decaying animal and plant matter, which dissolves to form a weak solution known as carbonic acid.

The ground water soaking through the cracks and joints of the limestone layers set up a gradual but inevitable chemical reaction. The original fissures were extended and enlarged and the slightly acid water, working away both at the inside and the outside of the rock, reduced it in places from a hard, solid mass into material of a soft, crumbling consistency. Naturally, the water, with its relatively low acid content, affected only small areas of limestone and that only slowly, but once begun, the corrosion process was unrelenting.

The slow corrosive action led to another. As the joints and bedding planes expanded, they allowed the

entry of more water, as well as sand, soil, gravel, stones and other debris. The combined action of fast-flowing water and the grinding, abrasive effect of the grit and pebbles carried in its wake, resulted in a further wearing down of the limestone and a widening of the intersecting channels. This activity is known as corrasion.

The dual processes of corrosion and corrasion, the rate and extent of which are of course dependent on such outside factors as rainfall amounts and climatic fluctuations, were largely responsible for the formation of today's limestone caves. After hundreds of thousands of years, the original narrow faults and joints had been opened out into a network of subterranean channels, and the abrasive materials carried by the underground streams had scoured regular beds in the rock. Their flow would sometimes be intensified by trickles from the rock walls and the appearance of subsidiary streams, until they swelled into raging torrents with stones and huge slabs of rock cutting out deeper channels.

The power of underground rivers, unable to dissipate their force by overflowing their banks, is often sufficient to cause the collapse of cave roofs and walls. Similar breakdowns may be caused by earthquakes or, at high altitudes, overwhelming weight of ice. Collapses of roofs may also occur as a result of natural stresses, where the surface layer is thin or where the arch supporting the cavity below is worn away by erosion. Sometimes such rock falls completely block the cave passage. Where they are piled so high that they touch the roof they are known as boulder chokes. Elsewhere such falls may result in an enlargement of a passage or vertical shaft so as to encourage rather than impede further progress.

No two caves are exactly alike in shape or size. Their individual features are determined by a variety of factors, the direction of bedding planes, faults and joints, the composition of the enclosing rock, the flow of ground water and its corrosive and corrasive properties. Broadly speaking, however, most caves contain a labyrinth of passages, shafts and chambers.

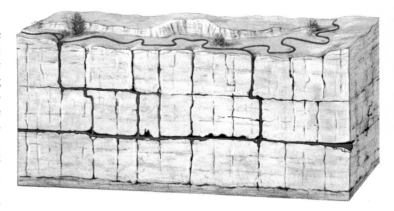

A passage is a more or less horizontal channel eaten or cut out of the surrounding rock by water action, whose shape is sometimes determined by the deposits of clay, silt, calcite and so forth, carried by the current. Main passages frequently follow the line of bedding planes and may slope upwards or downwards. The action of water may also cause some passages to be wider than they are high, and others to open out into high but narrow canyons.

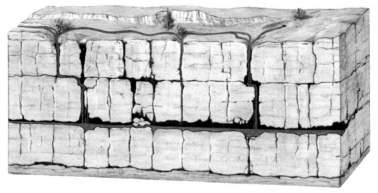

Shafts are similar to passages but have developed in a vertical direction, sometimes open to the sky, sometimes deep within a cave system. They are usually cylindrical or cone-shaped and markedly wider than the passages leading into or away from them.

Where a passage opens out to make a much larger cavity it is described as a chamber. It may attain huge proportions, with ample space for decorative formations, and is often situated at the point

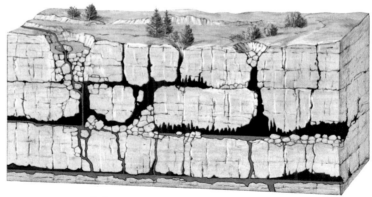

This series of pictures shows how limestone caves are formed. Rain and ground water percolate through the joints in bedding layers, the dilute carbonic acid dissolving the limestone. The joints expand and larger cavities form. Calcite stalactite formations grow from the roof, which often collapses under various pressures. Eventually, at a deeper level, the water flows through an active cave as a river, emerging at a karstic spring.

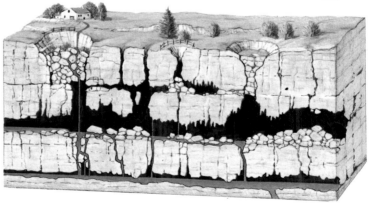

Huge blocks of rock break off from the cave roof. Sometimes a barrel vault, capable of bearing the strain, is formed.

constantly flowing, are always liable to alteration and new growth. It is these caves, with their underground streams, rivers, pools and lakes, and their weird and beautiful natural formations, that attract most speleologists.

There are other theories about cave formation in addition to the mechanical processes already described. When the surface water seeps down to what is known as the "water table"—that is, the layer of water below the earth's surface—it has obviously reached its lower limits. The rock below is saturated and the ground completely waterlogged. The zone below the water table is called the *phreatic,* and the zone above the *vadose.* Caves formed below and above the water table take their respective names from these zones.

Some experts dispute this theory, arguing that if a channel is full of water, phreatic features will develop regardless of height above or below the water table. Thus the water table height varies according to fissure size and water flow.

Vadose caves that have been formed by corrosion and corrasion are often T-shaped in cross-section; but phreatic caves, formed below the water table, normally lack the ridges and bends brought about by corrasive action. The corners of these caves are fairly smooth and rounded, and the cavities themselves more or less circular in cross-section. Some caves, however, have a keyhole-shaped cross-section, the upper portion being circular and phreatic, the lower section narrow and trench-like, cut out by a vadose stream as the water table, affected by seasonal changes, became lower.

Some of the limestone cave systems carved out by these various methods over hundreds of thousands of years are of staggering size.

Hard pebbles whirled round by the water grind out holes in the cave floor, the largest of them several yards in width.

where a number of passages converge.

In "dead" caves, the streams that helped to form them have gradually dried up and the beds, while clearly visible, are empty. Apart from further collapses of roofs and walls, such caves are unlikely to change structurally in the future. But "live" or "active" caves, where water is

This section of the Hölloch is elliptical in shape, indicating that the water has been active along the entire bedding plane.

The Flint Ridge system in Kentucky is almost 73 miles long and the Hölloch in Switzerland over 64 miles. Further expeditions may well succeed in extending these lengths. The deepest cave in the world is still the Gouffre de la Pierre Saint-Martin (3,872 feet), with the Gouffre Berger running it close at 3,755 feet. And enormous chambers, such as the largest of the Carlsbad Caves and the Grotta dei Giganti, near Trieste, are high enough to accommodate cathedrals!

St Peter's, Rome, would fit into Europe's largest cave, the Grotta dei Giganti.

Wind and ice caves

Caves formed by wind action alone are not common, but may sometimes be encountered in deserts or on mountain slopes. Strictly speaking, they are moulded under the bombardment of tiny particles of sand and grit swept along by winds travelling at high speeds. Anyone caught on a stretch of beach in a high wind can get a vague idea—from grains of sand stinging legs and arms—of the impact of minute wind-driven particles against a solid surface. In a desert sandstorm, with winds exceeding 60 miles an hour, the force is enormously magnified. Over an extended period, the particles grind deep hollows into the soft sections of rock exposed to the full fury of the storm, and wind caves are formed.

Caves may sometimes be formed by earthquakes and landfalls. Faults open at right angles to a slope, or cavities are found under the debris. Such covered caves are irregular in shape and highly dangerous, for the surrounding debris is not neatly stratified and is often on the verge of collapse. There are covered caves beneath rock falls in central Australia, which have been decorated as holy places by the aborigines.

Finally, a word about ice caves. These are naturally only found at high altitudes, in the Himalayas, Alps, Pyrenees, etc. or in regions of perpetual ice, such as parts of the Arctic and Antarctic. Some are formed entirely of ice, with spectacular icicles and waterfalls, others are icy only in winter when water pouring in is instantaneously frozen into fantastic formations.

The Eisriesenwelt (Giant Ice World), 5,400 feet up in the Austrian Alps, is the most famous and beautiful example of a perennial ice cave system. The ice never melts,

even in summer, and the low temperature rapidly freezes any snow filtering inside. As the visitor will quickly notice, the air is continually circulating. The total length of the cave system is over 25 miles, the largest single chamber being the Cathedral, named after the caves' first explorer, Alexander Mork. Visitors are conducted through with carbide lamps, for there is no other form of lighting available.

Another especially remarkable ice cave is the Grotte Casteret in the Pyrenees, named after the famous French speleologist who discovered it. Situated at a height of almost 8,000 feet, far higher than any Alpine cave, its temperature too is usually kept well below freezing point by icy blasts of wind. The huge ice-floor of the main hall was estimated by Casteret to measure over 3,300 square yards, and beyond it he found an immense subterranean glacier, with an area two and a half times greater than that of the hall.

Exploration of ice caves demands more than average courage and stamina, but it provides a unique experience.

Above: *tumbling rocks may form caves.*

Left: *wind and sand have moulded smooth hollows in the surface of Ayers Rock in central Australia.*

Below: *magic signs such as these on the wall of Ayers Rock are intended to exorcize gods and spirits.*

CHAPTER 5

THE SPECTACULAR
UNDERGROUND WORLD

Illusory treasure

Despite the alluring accounts of myths and fables, caves are not ideal hunting grounds for treasure seekers. Prospects of discovering large quantities of gold or other precious minerals below ground are remote, so speleologists are unlikely to make their fortunes that way. But any one who is content to stand and gaze, to yield to the spell of sheer wonder and beauty, will be amply rewarded in quite another sense, for the natural splendours of his surroundings are rarely equalled in the world of everyday life. Not without reason have cave explorers resorted to such terms as "wonderland" and "fairyland".

Most people have read about the spectacular cave formations known as stalactites and stalagmites, the long tube-like growths, similar to icicles, which hang down from cave roofs and rear up from the floor. Nobody going into a cave for the first time can fail to be impressed by their magnificence. But disappointment awaits any person misguided enough to try to break off one of these structures and take it away as a souvenir. For no sooner is it exposed to the dry air outside the cave than it begins to turn pale and lose shape. If it is left to lie around in the open, rain water attacking its surface will gradually cause it to dissolve completely, reversing the processes which formed it in the course of many centuries.

Stalactites and stalagmites are the most common types of sinter or calcareous formation to be found in limestone caves. They are also known as dripstone formations because they are partially the result of the continuous dripping of water on rock for thousands of years. We have seen how percolating rain water dissolves carbon dioxide from the air and soil, forming carbonic acid solution. This dissolves the limestone, forming a weak solution of calcium carbonate. On encountering the cave atmosphere, which contains smaller concentrations of carbon dioxide than the gases in the soil, the carbon dioxide comes out of solution. The water is no longer able to dissolve all the calcium carbonate, which is left in the form of precipitation. A thin deposit of lime remains on the cave roof or wall or drops to the floor, as a ring of crystallized calcite.

The crystals gradually grow into a slim tubular formation. When the tube hangs vertically down from the roof, it is known as a stalactite. Calcite deposits from water dripping down on to the floor and grow-

Irregular dripstone formations are known as eccentrics, as illustrated here in a cave at Erlach in Lower Austria.

Calcite layers have built up these deposits on a cave floor, following the courses of running water. Traces of iron have coloured them brown.

grotesquely shaped like an onion or a carrot, or twisted and spiralling like a corkscrew. Although the surfaces are usually smooth, the edges may sometimes be as sharp as blades.

Strange sizes and shapes

There are clearly many different factors at work in moulding stalactites into such unusual shapes. These must include the size and incline of the original aperture, the rate and direction of the water seepage, the amount of acid in the water, the temperature and humidity content of the cave, the influence of air currents and so forth. Converging streams of water along a sloping cave roof will obviously lead to rapid stalactite growth, while an isolated, narrow opening will be a limiting factor. It would seem that very slender, tubular stalactites have not been subjected to any form of atmospheric disturbance, while a steady and unvarying flow of air will cause them to bend from the true. And although stalactite development is normally a process lasting centuries, inspection of deserted wartime air raid shelters has revealed surprisingly rapid stalactite growth. Thus some of the environmental factors already mentioned may encourage an abnormally fast growth rate.

ing upwards are called stalagmites. Their growth pattern is similar but they tend to be thicker at the base, and altogether less streamlined. Both formations may take thousands of years to develop, with growth sometimes restricted to only a few inches in a century, the stalagmites being the slower growing of the two types. Sometimes the two formations join together to form a column, with a steadily increasing circumference.

The simple dripping of water, however, is not enough to explain the innumerable strange forms adopted by these dripstone growths, nor to determine why they display different rates of growth under varying conditions. Some stalactites are hollow while others are solid. Some are as thin as straws, others are cone-shaped or tapering, sometimes with a central tube as an extension of the original calcite rim. They may be

Stalagmites on the whole exhibit less variety in shape since they are almost exclusively dependent upon the water dripping from above. They are usually round and massive, with thick bases, but occasionally they too will rear up like slim pipes and tree trunks. Often they may resemble giant cakes or mushrooms, and sometimes they are steeply tiered, with clearly defined thin and thick sections which provide a clue to their overall pattern of growth.

When water runs down sloping walls or rock surfaces, attractive calcite formations known as flowstone may be formed. These often link together to form delicate, transparent curtains, waves and waterfalls.

Certain stalactite formations appear to have begun to develop in the normal manner but have suddenly branched and twisted out from the main growth in the most extraordinary fashion. Often they double back on themselves to form the most curious patterns, the overall effect being of an untrained plant or unpruned tree. Such malformed stalactites have been given different names, such as helictites, anemolites or eccentrics. Equivalent strange effects can also be seen in stalagmites and these are called heligmites. Various explanations have been put forward for this haphazard kind of development—windblown water and distorted crystal formation, for example—but no completely convincing reason has so far been found.

Other cave deposits

Stalactites, helictites and stalagmites comprise the most spectacular of all cave decorations, but there are other interesting formations, less familiar to the average visitor. Rimstone pools, also known as gours, are small ponds which collect on cave floors. They are formed

Above right: *in tunnels used as air raid shelters, twenty years have produced these slim, tubular stalactites and grotesque twisted helictites.*

Below right: *stalactites in the Hölloch resemble clubs and turnips.*

Right: *hollow tree-like formations in the Bärenhöhle.*

Reddish banners and small tubes of dripstone in the Hölloch.

from loss of carbon dioxide as water flows over the rim of a pool in a thin film. Calcite is deposited at the edge where the film of water is thin. Sometimes, particularly where the floor slopes, these gours build up into a series of steps or waves.

Cave pearls are formed by grains of sand or grit, encased in a calcite covering. This is the result of water dripping from the cave roof or trickling down a wall into a hollow, where it churns up the grains and eventually builds up a calcite coating round them. This layer may thicken until the object grows to the size of a golf ball. Sometimes it is perfectly smooth and round, at others rough in texture and of irregular shape. The name is slightly

misleading, for, as their constituent parts indicate, they have no intrinsic value.

Another formation often found in limestone caves is moonmilk. This, unlike the others mentioned, is not a crystalline deposit, but a soft, powdery substance, found alike on walls, roof and floor. Water would not seem to play any significant part in its formation and it is believed to be caused by bacterial action.

Some caves contain quantities of gypsum, and gypsum crystals, either flake-like or growing in the guise of clusters of white flowers, often decorate cave walls, roofs and stalactites. They too are formed as a result of water seeping through cracks in the rock.

Speleologists still have much to learn about the growth of these dripstone or sinter formations, and scientific research continues. An American biologist, for example, recently came across fungal threads in water droplets that had formed at the end of growing stalactites. The tiny threads bound together the lime crystals of the stalactite and the conclusion was that the fungi, themselves living on minute organisms in the percolating water, were playing an important role in the stalactite development. Under certain conditions, therefore, it is likely that bacteria are partially responsible for sinter growth, as in the case of moonmilk.

Dating the past

The scientific investigation of stalactites and stalagmites can also supply much valuable information about the past. Comparison of their structure in different caves, for instance, may reveal something about a region's former climate.

Annual fluctuations in rainfall

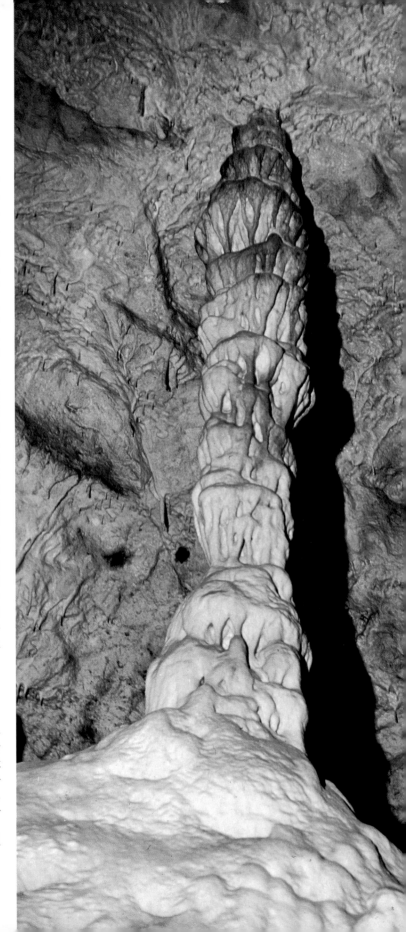

This huge stalagmite from the Nebelhöhle resembles a tree trunk in cross-section, with variously coloured growth rings.

and water supply are often reflected in the growth pattern of dripstone formations. In winter, when the soil is frozen, the flow of water ceases, resuming once more in the spring and continuing into the summer and autumn. The annual miracle of new life and growth, unleashed by the combination of sunlight, warmth and moisture, finds its small responsive echo in the sunless world below ground. The life processes of animals and plants around and immediately above the cave are intensified. These increase the dissolving properties of ground water entering the cave and in turn stimulate continued calcareous growth.

Indeed, if a cross-section is cut through an ordinary stalactite, a series of concentric rings will be visible, comparable to those found in a similar section of a tree trunk. The rings are wide and narrow, dark and light. A longitudinal section taken from a stalagmite will also reveal the patterns of caps lying above one another, indicating distinct periods of slow and rapid growth.

To the trained observer, the stalactite and stalagmite calendar can sometimes help to date the origin of the cave itself. But considerable skill and caution is required to interpret this correctly, for each stalactite is a separate individual, whose history may differ even from that of its immediate neighbour. It is extremely difficult to say positively whether the sinter represents an original formation or whether it is the result of later contributory factors—such as a crack opened up by an earthquake, a volcanic eruption, a storm or a rock collapse.

Stalactites and stalagmites are ordinarily found in all the main sections of a normal cave system—in potholes, passages and chambers

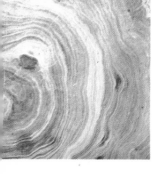

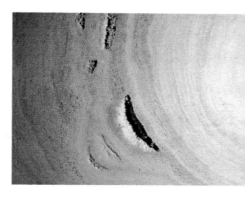

—but no two sites are exactly alike. Stalactite and stalagmite growth are demonstrably affected by the prevailing climate, the amount of annual rainfall and the density of plant cover on the surface. In temperate zones, cold and warm periods, wet and dry seasons alternate—and have done for hundreds of thousands of years. All such contributory factors may be reflected in dripstone growth, but climatic history alone cannot precisely date its age.

The radiocarbon tests

The only reliable method is radiocarbon dating, a recently perfected technique which can today be applied to every branch of geological and archaeological study, from rocks, trees and minerals to prehistoric pottery and tools, and Egyptian mummies.

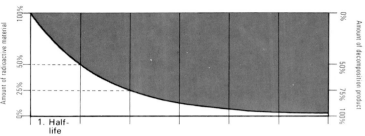

The activity of any given preparation of radioactive carbon (C^{14}) is reduced by one half in 5,568 years. Half of the remaining half decays within the next 5,568. This is how the half-life curve is formed.

Briefly, the method works as follows. A very minute quantity of carbon found in atmospheric carbon dioxide is radioactive, formed from nitrogen as a result of high-energy cosmic radiation. It has an atomic weight two units higher than that of ordinary carbon (whose chemical formula is C^{12}) and is thus called C^{14}.

This radioactive carbon is subject to decay. If an exactly known quantity of C^{14} were to be enclosed in a container, precisely half the number of its atoms would have decayed after 5,568 years. This is called its half-life.

A certain amount of radioactive carbon therefore enters percolating water and plays its part in the dissolution of limestone rock. It can be detected and isolated in calcareous tufa and dripstone formations. It is then a problem of measurement and calculation. If, for example, a fragment of stalactite were found to contain exactly half as much radiocarbon as was detected in a recently formed stalactite, it would be possible to date it as 5,568 years old—equivalent to the half-life of the radiocarbon. If it contained less, the conclusion would be that it was even older than that,

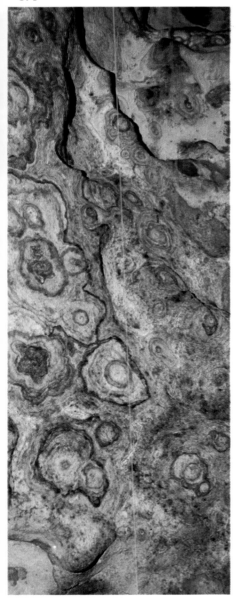

The stalactites have been broken off, possibly due to an earthquake, leaving only the starting points of the growth rings. The green patches are algae.

The Bue Marino Cave in Sardinia has a fantastic display of eccentrics.

cave off the island of Kefallinia (Cephalonia) in the Ionian Sea proved to have originated between 16,000 and 20,000 years ago. In the majority of European caves, however, the stalactites are of more recent development, a mere 3,000-4,000 years old. Since then, possibly as a result of a cooling climate, stalactite growth appears to have slowed down considerably.

Sometimes traces of other radioactive materials are found in caves, including uranium. Some stalactite fragments from a cave in southern France were successfully dated by microscopic examination of signs of disturbance caused by disintegrating particles of uranium. Apparently it began to grow about 130,000 years ago, stopping 40,000 years later, at the end of the last warm interglacial period. Comparative measurements of other sinter formations have confirmed that the glaciers returned about 70,000 years ago, before retreating once more to their present positions some 60,000 years later.

Broken stalactites can also act as natural seismographs to record past earth tremors and similar disturbances. The position of the fall can indicate the general direction and intensity of the impulse, and the approximate date of the occurrence, ascertained by using the normal radiocarbon method.

if more it must have been of later formation. In either case—provided the C^{14} content of air and soil carbon dioxide has not changed—the date could be ascertained with a fair degree of accuracy.

The age of the earth

This revolutionary scientific method has already upset many conventional and previously accepted theories about the probable age of the earth itself and the periods and localities in which different forms of life existed. In most instances, radiocarbon tests have shown organic matter to be far more ancient than had been supposed, of crucial significance in geology, palaeontology, archaeology and related fields.

Radiocarbon examination has clearly shown certain calcareous formations to be as much as 50,000 years old. Specimens of stalactites which were taken from a submarine

Subterranean wonderlands

Dripstone displays of stalactites, stalagmites and flowstone are the central features of show caves all over the world, and the careful positioning of concealed artificial lighting sets them off to spectacular advantage. In the magnificent Yugoslav caves of Postojna, for example, where visitors travel by miniature railway deep into the heart of the mountain and then continue their

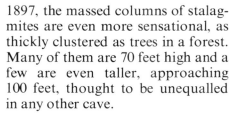

journey on foot, every grotto and chamber contains a new and surprising revelation. The stalactites and stalagmites are contorted into a myriad of strange and beautiful shapes. Imagination can run riot here, but in many instances suggestive names have been given, such as the Pulpit, the Leaning Tower of Pisa, the Palm Tree, the Crocodile, the Tortoise and the Lion's Head. Each of the immense caverns—the Cathedral, the Ballroom, the Concert Hall, the Paradise Grotto, the Black Chamber and the like—have their individual atmosphere. In places, the stalagmite columns rear up to 40 or 50 feet. Nor is this wonderful subterranean world without colour, for the minerals embedded in the rock glimmer and flash with every hue in the rainbow.

The Postojna Caves deservedly rank as one of the wonders of Europe. Yet in the United States, the giant Carlsbad Cavern rivals it both in size and splendour. In this, the largest cave in the world, miles of concealed lighting reveal colossal stalactites and stalagmites, many of them hung with crystals, sparkling and gleaming like an enormous horde of treasure. Here too each cavern has been given a descriptive name—Big Room, King's Palace, Queen's Chamber, Green Lake Room, Chinese Temple, etc. In the Big Room one huge stalagmite measures 62 feet tall, with a circumference of about 16 feet.

In the Aven Armand, in the French Pyrenees, discovered in

1897, the massed columns of stalagmites are even more sensational, as thickly clustered as trees in a forest. Many of them are 70 feet high and a few are even taller, approaching 100 feet, thought to be unequalled in any other cave.

Huge calcite basins in the Postojna Caves, and tiny conches in a stalactite in the Falkenstein Cave.

Centre right: *clints and karst tables in the Märenbergen, Switzerland.*

Below right: *a luxuriant plant growth at the surface intensifies the dripstone development in the cave below.*

The Judge's Court in the Eiskogel Cave, Austria.

Clints and grikes

Water acting on limestone terrain also creates some unusual outdoor formations. Deep trenches and lacerations are often seen on limestone plateaux in mountainous areas. They are known by various local names, including clints—pavements with criss-cross grooves—and grikes, deep vertical grooves in the clints. Many of these trenches run in the same general direction as rock fissures, others have been incised into the rock surface by running water. Standing water too, even on a horizontal plane, may cut out deep basins and sinkholes.

In the Swiss Alps, individual limestone blocks may sometimes be found scattered about an otherwise level plain, often jutting up 30-40 feet. These were left behind on the limestone surface when the glaciers retreated about 10,000 years ago. Although the surrounding terrain has slowly and steadily been dissolved, the slabs have protected the rocks below from erosion. The approximate dissolution rate over that period has been calculated so that these blocks, perched high above the surface, can also provide scientists with clues as to the age of the neighbouring caves.

The cave wind

At one spot in the Postojna Caves the stalactites hang like rows of banners from the roof, yet strangely, not in the normal vertical position. Here is undisputed evidence of the action of the wind inside the cave bending the dripstone formations as they grow. The seeping water, fanned by the wind, leaves limestone deposits on the lee side so that the stalactites project at an angle instead of growing straight down.

All cavers know how powerful the cave wind can be, creating waves on underground lakes and, annoyingly, blowing out acetylene lamps. In some mountain regions it may attain a force of up to 30 miles per hour. Often there is a steady gale inside the cave, elsewhere the frequency and rate of the wind depend on outside air pressure.

The force of the cave wind is something that must be taken into careful consideration by all potholers planning a lengthy stay underground, for it can create very unpleasant conditions.

Air temperature inside the cave system affects dripstone growth. If the cave temperature is warmer than the outside temperature, the lighter cave air ascends and cold air is sucked into the lower sections. If the outside temperature rises, the air circulation pattern is reversed and heavy cold air flows out of the cave entrance. When a cave system in a high mountain region is linked

Winds blow in and out of the vast entrances to Alpine caves, depending on the state of the weather and the temperature.

by a shaft with the surface, air streaming down into the cave is cold. Thus the temperature in such caves is usually about the same as the outside mean temperature, leading in winter to extensive formations of ice.

A large cave system is therefore subject to vigorous ventilation, but smaller caves with a single entrance may also be affected by the movements of cold and warm air masses. Cave organisms learn to adapt themselves to these changing conditions. Bats, for example, have been observed covered with drops of dew as they hang from a roof about 30 feet from the entrance. At night, as the cave temperature dropped, so too did the animals' body temperatures. In the morning, the sun warmed the air at the cave entrance and as the warm air was sucked in along the ceiling the cold cave air was ejected. The moisture in the warm air was then deposited as dew on the fur of the sleeping bats.

A mouse-eared bat covered with dew in a cave entrance.

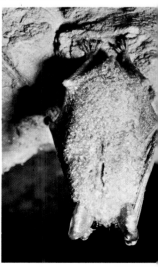

CHAPTER 6

THE DISAPPEARING RIVERS

Underground water

The limestone regions generally described as karst are found both in the Old and New Worlds, although, as already mentioned, it is a term specifically applied to the northern Dalmatian coast region of Yugoslavia. The word itself comes from the Serbo-Croat tongue. Karst terrain has certain main distinguishing features—an abundance of large caves and underground rivers, and, above the surface, extensive stretches of barren, rocky ground, laced with depressions. These include potholes, clints and grikes, sinkholes and basins (known locally as *polja*)—all of which are directly or indirectly caused by water action —and *dolines*, which are depressions caused by solution or resulting from the collapse of a cave roof situated near to the surface.

In typical karst regions, surface streams and lakes are exceptional, the reason being that most of the rainfall sinks rapidly into the porous limestone and vanishes underground. Fresh water, therefore, is often a luxury in many of these arid regions. Yet often, after tunnelling out an intricate network of channels below ground, streams and rivers suddenly bubble out as springs or even flow above the surface for a

short distance, only to disappear again into the depths. The connection between these streams and rivers has not always been evident, but modern scientific techniques now indicate that what were previously considered to be separate and disconnected currents may often prove to be part of the same river.

The scientific study of underground water by hydrologists has a special importance for everyone living in the neighbourhood. Not only can it contribute to our further knowledge of cave systems, but it also has a significant effect on soil erosion and fertility, drainage and fresh water supply, all crucial to life in a rural community. Everything related to such water is vital and easily ascertained—direction, temperature, rate of flow, volume, seasonal variation and chemistry.

The Danube and the Aach

Encyclopaedias, no two of which exactly agree, give the total length of Europe's River Danube as around 1,770 miles. But an aerial survey of the great river would show that it is by no means visible along its entire length, from its source in the Black Forest mountains of southwestern Germany to its outlet in a great delta on the Black Sea.

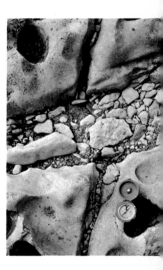

Clefts in the limestone of the Danube bed, formed by rock displacements, are clearly visible.

The Danube seeps away at Fridingen, shortly after it rises in the mountains of the Black Forest.

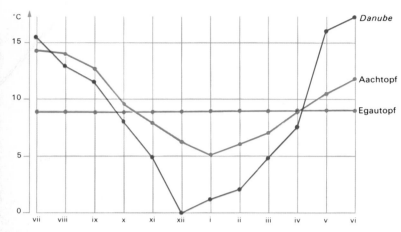

Comparisons of the temperature changes of the Danube (blue), the Aachtopf (green) and the Egautopf (red), indicates the close relationship between the Danube and the Aach. Their temperature curves are remarkably similar.

Fed by some 300 tributaries, it is over 300 yards wide as it flows past Vienna, and a bare 450 feet above sea level. In other places it broadens out to almost a mile, often flooding the surrounding countryside. Below Ulm it is navigable to medium-sized craft, but along its upper course it frequently narrows until it is little wider than a stream, and from time to time it completely vanishes underground.

In fact, the river disappears in the limestone of the Swabian Alps

barely nineteen miles after it rises. Except during particularly wet years, the water vanishes through joints in the river bed and banks, pursuing a meandering course below ground and finally emerging downstream, not, as might be expected, in its original and clearly traceable bed, but in a great spring at the source of the Aach river, a tributary of the Rhine flowing into Lake Constance.

The water surges out at this point at a great speed, and whereas many similar springs are crystal-clear, the water of the Aach, when in flood, tends to be loamy and yellowish. Its temperature also records considerable variations according to season. In summer it may rise to about 59°F (15°C) whereas in winter it will drop to around 41°F (5°C). In fact, the characteristic variations in colour, temperature and flow all reflect, though in less dramatic fashion, the behaviour of the Danube itself.

Early investigations into the hidden underground course of the Danube led to many false conclusions, but the Danube-Aach connection was eventually confirmed. At high water it takes about 20 hours for the main river to reappear at the Aach spring, at low water approximately three times as long.

In theory, it might be possible to block up all the holes and fissures in the bed of the Danube so as to provide an adequate water supply for all the villages and towns of the upper Danube valley. Such a procedure would, however, seriously disrupt the operations of mills and factories along the Aach. In the past there has been much dispute among the different local authorities about the distribution of the Danube water, but agreement has now been reached whereby the flow of the two interconnected rivers will be

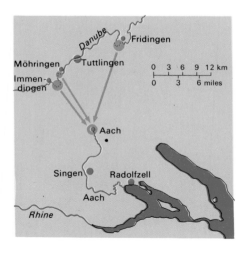

A map of the area where the Danube disappears and its relationship to the Aach spring.

regulated in such a way that power is fairly divided in all areas.

The first attempts to trace the course of the Danube were made with the aid of ordinary domestic salt, which was tipped into the water at the point where it seeped away under the ground, and was subsequently detected at the point of emergence. This rather hit-and-miss method has now been superseded by simpler and more accurate scientific techniques. Minute traces of salt in water can be detected by chemical means through a spectrophotometer, in which a colourless flame turns yellow in the presence of sodium. For continuous observation over a long period, an automatic recorder may be used to measure the water's electrical conductivity. The larger the salt content, the greater the conductivity.

Other types of marker apart from cooking salt can also be used—potassium salts, for instance, which colour a flame lilac. But the method most widely employed by hydrologists nowadays is a coloured dye, such as fluorescein, which is both easy to handle and to see. The dye dissolves in water to form a greeny-yellow solution, so that even when diluted to one part in ten million, it can be detected by the naked eye. In ultra-violet light even smaller amounts of pigment can be measured, so that with special instruments it is traceable in a dilution of one part in 100 milliards. A mere two pounds of fluorescein is sufficient to treat a quantity of 20,000,000,000 gallons!

The Falkenstein Cave

This method was successfully used to produce some remarkable findings about underground water in the two-mile-long Falkenstein Cave in the Swabian Alps of Germany. This cave is fed by water from basins situated in undulating hill country about 2,000 feet above sea level. There are no signs of springs or streams but the presence of dolines suggests that there are caves under the plateau.

In the summer of 1960, a tanker flushed twelve cubic yards of water, treated with half a pound of fluorescein, into a doline on the dry hill top. Observation posts were set up at 30 springs in the vicinity and samples taken every few hours were sent through to a central laboratory.

Firemen wash fluorescein into a doline in the Swabian Alps.

Dolines are found in rows following the line of subterranean caves. Unfortunately they are often used for dumping waste, causing pollution of ground water.

There is a relationship between cave formation and valley development. The initial cave system is mainly dependent on the mountain structure. Once intersected by valleys, the gradient alters, usually leading to intensified corrosive action and cave enlargement. The original direction of slope survives for a long time. The vertical scale here is greatly exaggerated.

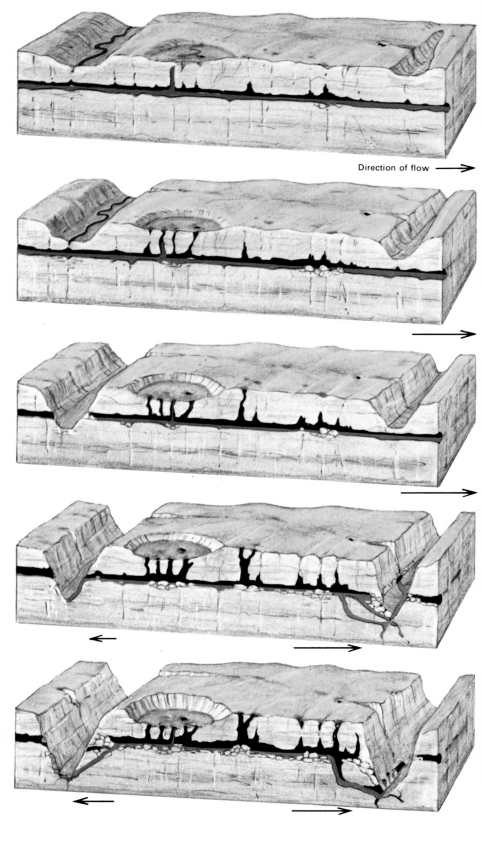

Direction of flow →

Although the springs were watched for two weeks, there was no trace of green dye. The failure of this first experiment was attributed to the exceptionally dry summer and the fact that insufficient quantities of water and dye were used.

The following year saw the experiment repeated, but this time with more water (26 cubic yards) and about two pounds of dye. Within 72 hours the stream in the cave had turned bright green. The water had moved at a rate of 37 yards an hour and most of it had flowed into the cave, although this was not the most direct route. A relatively small amount of water flowed by a shorter route in the opposite direction.

In the winter of 1964, the connection between these two outflows was shown even more clearly. The frozen soil was impervious to moisture and the water from the melting snow coursed in wide streams over the plateau and into the basin where the dyed water had been introduced three years previously. It formed a small lake, under the weight of which the new basin eventually collapsed. The lake water swirled down into the aperture and some four pounds of fluorescein was tipped into it. Only four hours later the stream surging out of the Falkenstein Cave appeared vivid green. The water's velocity had now, under flood conditions, increased to 750 yards an hour. The true velocity of the cave stream was nearer 1,000 yards an hour. Coloured water also flowed northward, in the opposite direction, at an increased speed.

Three conclusions were drawn by the hydrologists from this series of experiments. Firstly, the sheet of water pouring into the cave after the collapse of the doline flowed at a faster rate than any caver could run. The level of the water in the ravine-like cave then rose so rapidly that a trapped caver might only extricate himself by scrambling on to a high rock fall. Secondly, during periods of severe flooding, erosion of the outside surface could be expected to occur. Mud and soil would be carried by the flood waters through open dolines and shafts and be deposited in the caves below as loam. Thirdly, whereas the Falkenstein cave system was known to cross the hill from valley to valley, there was evidence of a more ancient cave system intersecting it. Further support for this theory was provided by the discovery, on the valley side facing the Falkenstein Cave entrance, of another entrance to an active cave.

The stream with many names

The unpredictable behaviour of underground streams and rivers in the karst region of northwest Yugoslavia has puzzled and fascinated local cavers and hydrologists. It was only as the result of experiments similar to those carried out near the Falkenstein Cave that it was recently discovered that five mountain streams, each with their separate names, were actually the same river.

In addition to the usual salt and dye tests, scientists introduced lycopodium (clubmoss) spores into the water. These spores, which are quite harmless, make a very fine dust that does not sink and which can be removed from the water with nets normally used for catching plankton. By dyeing lycopodium spores different colours, several sinks can be simultaneously tested.

Not far from the town of Ljubljana, a stream rises at a spring and crosses a typical polje—a basin with no outlet—until it reaches the limestone hills. There it suddenly disappears. Dye experi-

Collapse of a doline in February 1964 above the Falkenstein Cave.

The river with five names flows through a gorge under this great natural bridge, all that remains of an old cave.

ments have proved that the same water reappears in streams which rise to the other side of the hills, flowing on across fields and meadows through the basin of the Cerkniško, surrounded by grey limestone mountains. Eventually it vanishes into huge caves. Application of standard saline tests indicate that the same stream then surfaces in a gorge behind the mountain. Then, after a brief stretch above ground, the stream once more vanishes beneath the surface.

Lycopodium spores which were tipped into the stream as it rushed through the gorge were later found in the water of the cave river Unica, beyond the next range of hills. A short distance from this cave, the Unica is joined by another stream, the Pivka. This river rises in the hills adjacent to the Postojna Cave system, gathers in the broad Postojna valley basin, and meanders down to link with the Unica. Fluorescein tipped into the source waters of the Pivka and reappearing

Rivers and streams in the Postojna and Cerkniško regions. A many-branched river network develops above impervious subterranean areas. In the porous limestone there are virtually no river courses at the surface.

in the Unica provided conclusive evidence that the waters of the two rivers mingled at this point.

The Unica now proceeds to twist and turn in a northerly direction until it again disappears at the foot of another range of limestone hills. A short while later it surfaces for the last time, where it earns itself yet another local name—Ljubljanica—and then vanishes into a cave.

This peaceful pattern continues throughout the dry season and during the winter, when snow covers the karst region. But the scene is dramatically and violently transformed as soon as there is a heavy and continuous fall of rain or when the snows begin to melt. Now the excess amounts of water cannot be absorbed by the various fissures and sinkholes that criss-cross the rocky terrain and the flood level rises dangerously until it fills the entire basin. When spring arrives, there is a body of water, about two square miles in area, entirely made up of the accumulated water of the previous season—the famous Cerkniško Lake.

During the spring the local peasants catch fish in the newly-formed lake. In summer, as the water slowly filters away, they plough the fertile soil which remains behind. This convenient pattern was not always so predictable and regular. In the 18th century, blockage of the fissures resulted in the lake water remaining undrained for seven years, with widespread flooding. Similar unwelcome occurrences are easily averted nowadays by simply removing all wood, twigs and miscellaneous rubbish carried by the river, so that the water can escape in due course unhindered.

The river with many names is now fully plotted, and enthusiastic cavers have been able to follow its various subterranean links in boats or by a

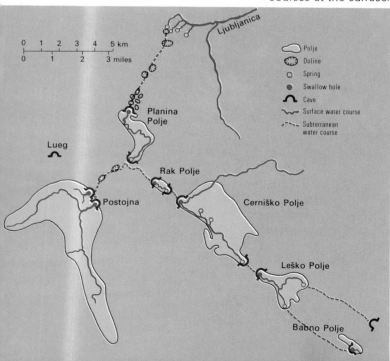

0 1 2 3 4 5 km
0 1 2 3 miles

Lueg

Ljubljanica

Planina Polje

Rak Polje

Postojna

Cerniško Polje

Leško Polje

Babno Polje

Polje
Doline
Spring
Swallow hole
Cave
Surface water course
Subterranean water course

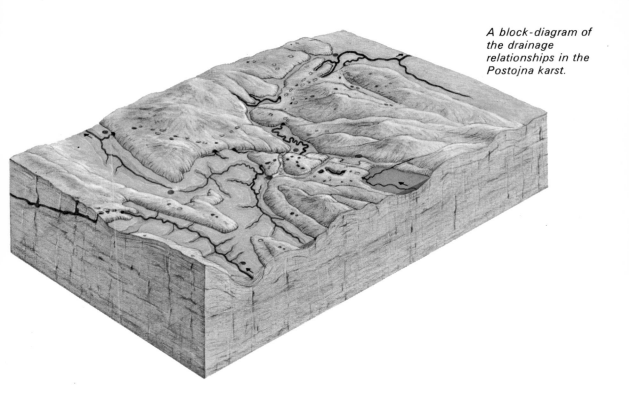

combination of climbing, swimming and diving, for considerable distances. Even the river's small tributary streams, which also follow winding underground courses, have been marked with dye and salt and allotted their proper place in the overall drainage pattern.

The eels of the Reka

Another famous stream flows in a southwesterly direction from the area of the Cerkniško Lake. It is called the Reka—actually the local name for "river". After pursuing a normal course for some distance, it plunges into a deep rock-strewn valley and then disappears into a cave. Farther on there is an enormous chasm where a doline has formed as a result of an earlier cave roof collapse. It is linked by a natural bridge with an even larger doline. From the edge of this chasm one can peer down, as through an immense window, at the Reka, bubbling and roaring 480 feet below. Then the raging torrent vanishes once more into the mountain side.

The river now surges through one of the largest and most complex cave systems in the valley. The local name is Škocjanske Jame—*jama* being the word for "cave". The stalactite-filled cave is an impressive enough spectacle. At one point the roof rises to about 360 feet and is lost in the darkness. Mist seeping into the cave provides an eerie and uncomfortable effect and far away, unseen, the roar of the subterranean river can be heard as it rages through the rocky bed of a deep gorge.

Enterprising cavers have managed to follow the underground course of the Reka for almost four miles, working their way round immense boulders which divert the natural flow of the river into thundering cascades. Beyond this point the roof descends to the level of the water and the river disappears into the darkness and uncharted depths. It is not always possible to follow the Reka as far as this. Sometimes the level of the water rises to flood the entire cave, and once, back in 1826, the river rose half-way up the sides of the doline outside, forming a lake 240 feet deep.

Scientists studying the course of the Reka hit upon an ingenious method of testing their theories. They loosed a number of specially marked eels into the stream at the point where it entered the caves. Some eight weeks later the eels were spotted swimming in the springs of the Timavo River, north of Trieste, after a leisurely 25-mile journey through the mountains. They had not troubled to keep pace with the river itself, for fluorescein-dyed water, introduced at the same point, took a mere ten days to reappear in the Timavo. It took the water only eight days longer to reach springs on the shores of the Adriatic Sea.

The force of the current of a river such as the Reka, at high water, is unimaginably powerful. It is capable of shifting giant rocks and boulders weighing more than a ton, while pebbles and smaller rock fragments are whirled around by the seething torrent and hurled like deadly projectiles against the cave walls. The river hurtling through its gigantic tunnel has been estimated to travel at speeds of up to nine yards a second—nearly 20 miles per hour—carrying with it immense quantities of mud, sand, loose rock and other debris. The cave has been dated at about a million years old, so that hydrologists have been able to do some interesting calculations, including the quantity of mud which the river must have dumped into the Adriatic in the course of all those centuries!

A block-diagram of the Škocjanske neighbourhood, showing the Reka and an older, disused course of the river. A cave passes below the village and downstream a small and large doline drain into the river.

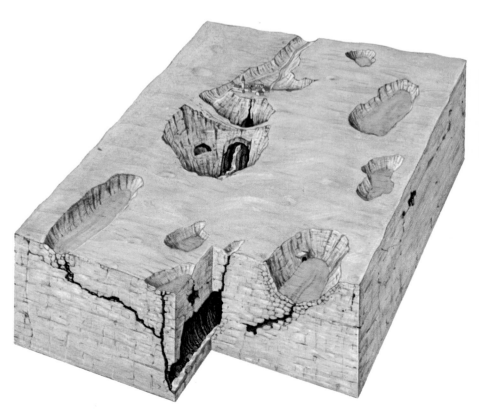

These various kinds of marking experiments, with and without eels, have significance for others besides the speleologists. One important and very practical result is the potential use of such underground streams and rivers for drinking purposes. Such water can only be considered for human consumption if the velocity of the stream is low enough to provide for the water to cleanse itself and for all rotting material to be decomposed. All potentially infective organisms and impurities must be entirely removed for the water to be safe for drinking. Chemical examination of water samples are essential to determine the pH content (the degree of acidity and alkalinity), the amount of dissolved salts, the bacteriological content and a variety of other relevant facts.

There have been instances of drinking water in mountain areas

Now that the water is polluted, many karst springs formerly used for the supply of drinking water are unusable. This can be clearly seen at high water when the water takes on a loamy colour, due to insufficient underground purification.

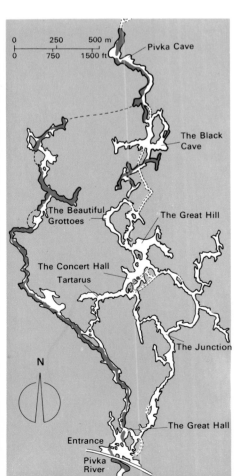

Left: *a map of the Postojna Caves.*

Quite simple means have been devised to conduct hardness and bacteriological tests in the open air.

suddenly beginning to smell of apple juice or tasting faintly of brandy as a result of an accidental leakage of a truck load somewhere in the hills. While both effects could be quite pleasant, there is a more serious side to the matter. The leakage could just have easily have been in the form of oil or sewage. Such risks to health are magnified daily wherever industry tightens its grip in formerly rural areas. Pollution, of which this is only one form, is a major problem of our time. Cave and hydrological research, such as has been described in this chapter, play their part in helping to maintain a safe and healthy environment.

CHAPTER 7

SUBMARINE CAVES

The search for fresh water

The *Medusa* is a little Greek fishing vessel, fifteen feet long, six feet wide, with a diesel engine, a small mast and a sail which protects the crew from the scorching rays of the mid-summer sun. Outwardly she looks no different from the hundreds of other fishing boats plying the coastal waters of the Ionian Sea, but the *Medusa* is not looking for fish. Instead, the group of geologists, physicists and engineers lining her deck are searching for fresh water.

The *Medusa* is scanning the sea in the area of Nauplia, a port on the Peloponnesian coast of Greece. The delicate instruments carried on board are capable of measuring the salinity of sea water to an accuracy of one-hundredth of one per cent. It is done by an electric recording device, the same as is used for measuring the salt content of under-ground streams and rivers. As the salinity of the water increases, so does its conductivity. During the course of a journey across, say, a

gulf near the mouth of a stream, continuous and automatic measure-ments can be recorded on a strip of paper, showing the exact proportion of salt to fresh water. The instru-ments are coupled to the *Medusa's* steering gear, so that the ship is automatically guided to those parts of the sea that contain the least amounts of salt. Inevitably, this

Right: *Fresh water gushing up in the Bay of Nauplia.*

Left: *a brackish water lake in the Melisani Cave on the east coast of Kefallinia.*

The supply of fresh water from the sea near Kiveri began in 1970.

brings her sooner or later to the mouth of a river.

In the height of summer, the rivers along this coast run dry. Even so, there are wide enough variations in the salt content of the coastal waters for the instruments aboard the research vessel to react sharply. Where the terrain is flat, she chugs in to within a few hundred yards of the shore; where there are cliffs, she may back off a mile or so. The instruments register strongly in these areas of "sweet" water, which is distinguishable from the surrounding sea water by being cooler and appearing more cloudy.

Ocean springs

In some places, almost pure water gushes powerfully up from depths of 60 to 90 feet to the surface. These submarine upsurgings cause extremely strong vibrations which rock the small boat violently and drive her outwards from the centre of the activity. Such sea springs have been known to fishermen

since ancient times. They are also very active along the Adriatic coast of Yugoslavia where they are known by the local name of *vrulje*, meaning "boiling water". And similar springs have recently been discovered off the coasts of Tunisia and Lebanon. The submarine springs off Lebanon are reported to be the most powerful yet known.

Springs of comparable size and force are of course found on land as well, but only in the vicinity of mountains with extensive cave systems. Their behaviour is similar to that of submarine freshwater springs, and a large-scale experiment carried out at the Aswan Dam in Egypt revealed some interesting facts. It was found that when the flow of the Nile was checked by the huge dam, the level of the water failed to rise as high as original calculations had predicted. This was due neither to an increase in the amount of water flowing beneath the dam nor to a higher rate of surface evaporation. Little attention had until that time been paid to the many ancient caves along the edge of the Nile valley. When the dam came to be built, it was found that a surprising proportion of the river water flowed through such caves to the Red Sea, emerging again from openings below sea level. It is possible that Nile water also flows westward under the Sahara, though this would be difficult to prove, as it would doubtless take years before it reappeared off the North African coast.

What then is the source of these natural underground springs? Certain conclusions can already be drawn. Leaves and other remains of plants discovered in submarine springs indicate that the water definitely has a land origin, and that it flows through a system of underwater caves to springs which have their outlets on the ocean floor.

Most of the Yugoslav sea springs provide cool water even in summer, the temperatures (50°-54°F or 10°-12°C) being similar to that of terrestrial cave water. These springs rise so strongly from their rocky beds that divers, even when weighted down, experience difficulty in finding the exit holes, and are forced up to the surface by the pressure of the water. Such huge springs indicate that entire rivers have sometimes been swallowed up by mountains, and there are many examples along the coast of Yugoslavia.

The changing sea level

Many springs, such as the Timavo, near Trieste, and the Ombla, near Dubrovnik, are at sea level or just above it. The existence of pure water springs on the sea floor is easier to comprehend when one remembers that since the last Ice Age, about 10,000 years ago, the sea level has risen 250-300 feet. Cave systems that had entrances at sea level during the Ice Age were therefore flooded at a later date. As the temperature rose, melting the ice caps of the Polar regions and mountain summits, the sea crept back to flood large portions of land, forcing the pure water streams back into the caves. With the former exits blocked, shafts that had once directed rain water into the caves now became possible exit routes for the spring water. But if the shaft was sufficiently large and there was also a sizeable quantity of water flowing down from the hinterland, the pressure of the sea water would prove inadequate to withstand the force of the accumulated ground water. Moreover, in ancient closed cave systems, there were comparatively few shaft-like openings in the roof through which water could escape, and thus the submarine springs became deeper and receded farther into the caves, and away from the shore. In such ways the old cave systems have been converted into virtual pipe lines of fresh water. In a few instances, a spring of fresh water has suddenly welled up on an island some distance from the coast of the mainland where the supply clearly originated.

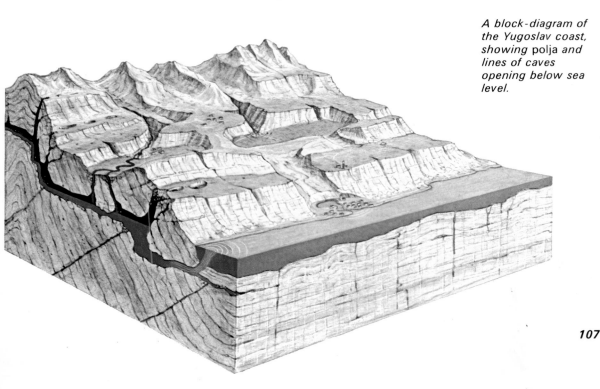

A block-diagram of the Yugoslav coast, showing polja *and lines of caves opening below sea level.*

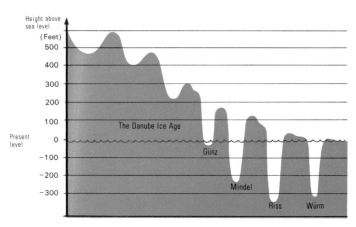

The Danube Ice Age

Günz

Mindel

Riss   Würm

Changes in the sea level between the Ice Age and today.

The sea mill of Argostólion

Caves drowned by the rising post-glacial seas and causing freshwater springs to gush under the ocean are one of the many fascinating aspects of speleological research. There are also unusual happenings related to coastal caves which are still well above sea level.

Near the town of Argostólion, on a rocky peninsula of the Ionian island of Kefallinia (Cephalonia), there is a great steel mill wheel. It is quite an ordinary wheel, except that it rotates in the wrong direction. The mill race carries the sea water past the mill and into a series of dark slits in the rock, some feet below sea level. Thus the water in the channel is flowing toward the land and not the sea, while the paddles beneath the mill wheel turn in the same direction. A barrier in front of the mill prevents too much water running through, maintaining the slight drop in level between the open sea and the holes in the rock.

The old mill on the peninsula was built alongside these shallow holes during the 19th century. A severe earthquake in 1952 destroyed it, but the sea water continued to be swallowed up in many places, some of them immediately offshore, at an estimated rate of 50 gallons per second. The present mill was then erected on the site of the old one.

To the casual observer, this is a strange phenomenon, although it is evident that the percolation is somehow related to a cave system. Austrian cave divers in fact proved that one group of caves on the island had been flooded since the Ice Age. In a cave not far inland from the east coast, they found a stalactite in brackish water, some 75 feet below sea level. Since drip-stone does not form under water, this was clear evidence that the cave had not been flooded during the last Ice Age. It is also known that the island of Kefallinia has not sunk since that period. So the divers proved conclusively that climate alters the sea level.

Conflicting theories

This discovery does not, however, explain the movement of water in this submarine cave system, and there has been a good deal of guess-work in this respect. One suggestion was that huge caves were slowly being filled with sea water. Yet as long as memory goes back, sea water has seeped in at Argostólion, so that even the largest imaginable caves would by now have been completely inundated. This explanation, therefore, is highly unlikely. A second theory claimed that dry clay and marl layers were sucking up the

This seaside mill was built in the 19th century at Argostólion. The mill stream runs in a landward direction.

Right: *after an earthquake had destroyed the old mill, it was replaced by this steel mill wheel, operating in the same manner.*

water. Apart from the fact that most of the island and its submarine plinth consists of limestone, the seepage has been going on for so long that this too seems most improbable. A third explanation was that the sea water sank until it met molten magma and evaporated.

Below: *there are stalactites deep below the sea surface in the water-filled caves of Kefallinia.*

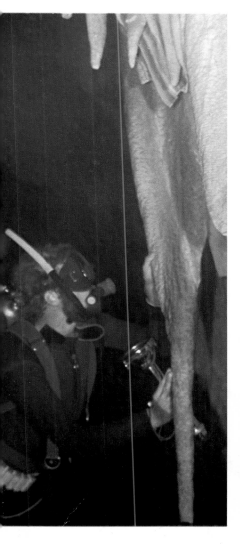

But there are no volcanoes in the vicinity where this could happen. The only possible conclusion could be that the percolating water did not remain underground, but re-appeared elsewhere. This indeed has now been shown to be correct.

Tracing the sea water

On the eastern side of the island is the cave where the divers discovered the submarine stalactite. The water of the lake inside this

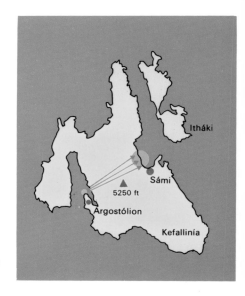

Brackish water springs are found both in the sea and along the coast.

cave is deep blue when the sun shines on it and, somewhat surprisingly, faintly salty in taste, though not nearly as markedly as sea water. Accurate measurements indicated a salt content of 0·03 per cent, which is in fact only about one-hundredth that of sea water. Could it be possible that the answer was being provided by the sea water percolating into the rock near the sea mill, 24 miles away on the opposite coast of the island, then being carried through natural underground pipes? Hydrologists set out to solve the mystery and establish a definite link.

The first attempt was a failure. About 90 pounds of fluorescein was used to try to trace the water's path. For eight days all the island springs were tested, without success. A later experiment in 1963 used four times the quantity of fluorescein. Fourteen days later, green water was reported in the cave on the east coast and shortly afterwards other springs along the coast showed the same signs.

The path of the water was now known, but one question remained to be answered. How did sea water entering at Argostólion three feet *below* sea level come to be flowing through caves two dozen miles away at a point three feet *above* sea level?

It is obvious that there must be an extensive and complicated cave system which provides a link between the east and west coasts of Kefalinia. But there is no positive indication of the manner in which the sea water from Argostólion moves under the ground. Sea currents and winds can certainly be ruled out completely. Neither does the natural ebb and flow of the tide play any significant part. If this were so, a change in the direction of the wind would cause the water at ebb tide to pour out of the swallow holes in the rock from time to time. Nothing like this has ever been observed. Nor can the cave system itself be visualized as functioning like a valve or an enormous suction pump. Such an arrangement would scarcely have survived the many very heavy earthquakes that have shaken the island over the centuries.

A matter of physics

There is a surprisingly simple explanation to the whole affair. The movement of the salt water in fact operates according to the elementary principle of communicating pipes. Think, for example, of an ordinary U-tube. If such a tube is filled with water from one side only, the water on the opposite side rises to exactly the same height. But if one side is filled with water and the other with oil, the level of the oil is higher than that of the water. The explanation for this is that a given quantity of oil is lighter than the equivalent quantity of water. Consequently, a shorter column of water is needed to balance a longer column of oil.

The cave system which runs below the island of Kefallinia can therefore be envisaged as an exaggerated

Salt water runs into the cave system in the west of the island and is joined by pure water under the mountains. On the east coast the mixed water rises and flows away three feet above sea level.

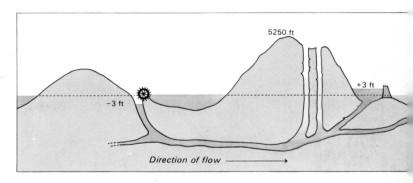

type of U-tube. The western portion of the tube is filled with salt water, the eastern section with brackish water, which is somewhat lighter in weight. This is why the mixed water in the caves along the east coast is three feet *above* sea level, whereas the infiltrating water from the sea at Argostólion is the same distance *below* sea level.

How deep are the caves?

This proven variation in comparative levels of six feet from east to west makes it possible to work out how far below the earth's surface the U-tube must extend. Since the relative densities of sea water and pure water are known, the answer can be calculated by simple mathematics, the only necessary modification being the fact that one is dealing with slightly brackish water instead of absolutely pure water.

We need not go into details, but the hydrologists calculated that in order to bring about the existing six-feet variation in water level between the point of entry and the lake outlet, the cave system would have to be approximately 210 feet below the surface. We have already seen that it is feasible for a cave to exist several hundred feet below sea level, bearing in mind that the level of the ocean has risen as much as 300 feet since the Ice Age.

During this process it is of course essential for some pure water to be present to dilute the sea water. This is available in the form of rain water which customarily falls in the mountain regions of the island, at a height of approximately 4,800 feet. This rain water then mingles with the sea water underground, some 200 feet down, and emerges as slightly brackish water.

Thus the sea mill of Argostólion, propelling salty water into the

In the Mediterranean, the roofs of great subterranean caverns sometimes collapse, forming sharp-edged dolines.

underground cave system of Kefallinia, clearly has more than a purely decorative function, capable of playing an important part in a natural pattern of drainage and irrigation. The builders of the old mill could hardly have known what was happening underground. The speleologists and hydrologists have now provided the answer.

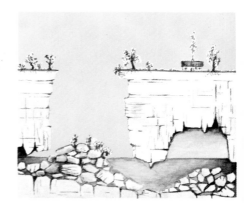

Fresh water from the sea

Now for a final glance at the fresh-water springs concealed under the sea. The marine springs in the neighbourhood of Nauplia are not entirely free of salt. So somewhere on the sea floor off the coast of the Peloponnese, there must be intakes that enable pure water to be mixed at depth with sea water.

Intensive study of the physical relationships of water currents in such submarine caves makes it possible for the water from these great marine springs to be collected, analyzed and used for domestic purposes. Collection of the water causes the level above the spring to rise, thus increasing the water pressure in the spring shaft. The level of the pure water therefore rises on the inflow side and the sea water is unable to follow it. In fact, the fresh water penetrates some distance into the area hitherto occupied by salt water.

In the experiments conducted aboard the *Medusa*, success ultimately depended upon this argument being correct both in theory and in practice. Tension increased as the instruments measured the change in salt content as the water rose up the pipe. Finally the scientists were proved right. Previously, the salt content of the water from the spring had been 0·2 per cent. Now the instruments showed that it had declined to 0·001 per cent.

Water from this source does not taste the faintest bit salty. And at a time when scientists everywhere are examining methods of extracting pure water from the oceans, this has shown itself to be a far cheaper technique than any other so far attempted. Fresh water from such sources can be used for irrigation purposes, for domestic consumption, for replenishing stocks of ground water and eventually for driving back sea water that has invaded coastal areas. It is yet another interesting example of the way in which science can exploit the processes of nature to benefit man.

Left: *a mass of debris dislocates the flow of the cave stream so that only divers can penetrate the inner chambers.* Below: *this collapse basin on the coast near Athens is a natural freshwater swimming pool.*

CHAPTER 8

THE WORLD'S GREAT CAVES

Clubs and study groups

Caving, both as a recreation and as a branch of geological study, attracts new enthusiasts every year. In those regions of the world where the most extensive limestone cave systems are to be found—in central and southern Europe and the United States—it is a highly organized activity, with numerous clubs and societies, many of them associated with universities which possess their own facilities for research in speleology and allied fields. In the United States and France, the activities of these individual clubs are co-ordinated on a national basis. Elsewhere, affiliations among local organizations are somewhat looser, although in most countries, including Great Britain, there are specialist groups collating, studying and publishing information of scientific importance and practical interest to cavers in their particular localities.

In other parts of the world, where important finds have already been made but where much still remains to be discovered, caving as a sport is either in a fairly early stage of development—as in Africa, Asia, Australasia and Central and South America—or its activities shrouded in silence, as in the Soviet Union and China.

Caves on show

Most of the really valuable work in speleology is done off the beaten track and away from the glare of mass-media publicity. But sometimes—as with an Altamira or a Lascaux discovery—reticence and modesty have to be thrown to the winds and the speleologists allowed to revel in their moments of glory. The great show caves of the world bear witness to their dedication, their skill and their courage, and it is right that the marvels they have uncovered should be shared with the public.

Every continent has its show caves, where visitors can be guided round in safety and comfort, on foot, in boats or in trains, to experience something of the majesty and awe of the subterranean world. They can listen to a Beethoven symphony in a natural concert hall or consume a three-course dinner in an air-conditioned restaurant—hundreds of feet below the ground.

The following brief survey of the main cave regions of the world is necessarily a highly selective one. There are, after all, upwards of 30,000 caves in the United States alone! So mention can only be made of a few caves of particular interest. In most cases, local names are

Large caverns in the Cottonwood Cave, New Mexico.

that it provided the foundations and stimuli for similar achievements in other parts of the world.

The painted cave regions

France boasts some of the most magnificent limestone caves anywhere, as well as the two deepest. In the Gouffre de la Pierre Saint-Martin in the Pyrenees, where the French caver Marcel Loubens fell to his death in 1952, an expedition sixteen years later established a new depth record of 3,872 feet. Almost as deep is the Gouffre Berger in the Isère region of the Savoy Alps (3,755 feet), while there are four others in France exceeding 1,500 feet.

Prehistorians have discovered a treasure store among the grottoes of Les Eyzies, where relics of human habitation have been proved to extend back to the Stone Age; and the painted caves of Lascaux, Laussel, Niaux, Marsoulas, Font-de-Gaume, Les Trois Frères, Montespan, Gargas, Rouffignac and others have revealed information of inestimable value concerning the social organization, cultural achievements and religious observances of early man.

Although the most splendid dripstone formations occur farther east, the stalactites in the caverns of the

The Concert Hall in the Jeita Cave, Lebanon.

Right: *polja on the Yugoslav coast.*

given, rather than their anglicized translations.

Undoubtedly, the most concentrated region of spectacular limestone caves is to be found in a broad belt stretching from northern Spain and southern France across Europe, by way of the French, Swiss, German, Austrian and Italian Alps, down to Yugoslavia. It is in these parts that caving had its beginnings, here that it registered its greatest tragedies and triumphs, and here

Grands Causses, especially the Aven Armand, Aven d'Orgnac and Gouffre de Padirac, are exceptionally fine. And the Grotte Casteret in the Pyrenees is by far the highest ice cavern in Europe.

Other famous examples of rock painting and engraving are found in Spain, both in the western Pyrenees (Altamira, Pindal, etc.) and, of a somewhat later date, in the Iberian mountain ranges of the eastern provinces. The Ojo Guareña cave in the province of Burgos is sixteen miles long. There are dry caves on the rock of Gibraltar and on the east coast of Majorca the decorative stalactites and subterranean lake of the Cueva del Drach are particularly noteworthy.

Echoes from mythology

Italy, an enthusiastic nation of cavers, possesses a number of impressive show caves in the southern Alps and in the karst area around Trieste. Here, on the border with Yugoslavia, is the Grotta dei Giganti, the largest underground cavern in Europe. Italy can also claim some of the deepest caves in the world—the Splugga della Preta (2,871 feet), the Grotta di Montecucco (2,648 feet), the Antro di Corchia (2,642 feet), and two others over the 2,000-foot mark.

South of Naples is the Grotta di Pertosa and, most celebrated of all, the Grotta Azzurra on the island of Capri. This cave, known in Roman times and rediscovered in 1826, can be reached only by boat, and its entrance lies partially below water. In the Apulia region, tourists enter and travel through the huge Grotta di Castellana by means of a chair lift.

The underworld, ruled by a sinister king, guarded by fierce

Circe's Chamber in the Eiskogel Cave.

Ice "clubs" in the
Eiskogel Cave.

monsters and populated by the spirits of the damned, features prominently in classical mythology and literature. If your imagination alone is not vivid enough to conjure up the shades of Polyphemus the Cyclops, of Hercules and the giant Geryon, of Charon the ferryman and three-headed Cerberus, local guides will gladly do it for you. But even if a lingering doubt remains as to whether a particular cave was really the original entrance to Pluto's kingdom, there is enough to exercise the fancy and delight the senses. Many of the limestone caves of the Greek mainland and islands are still below the present sea level, others, once flooded, now elevated above it. The Petralona Cave on the peninsula of Khalkidhiki contains a wonderful display of stalactites, and the entrance shaft of the Provatina Cave is the longest sheer, uninterrupted vertical drop in the world—no less than 1,298 feet straight down!

The great karstic caves

The limestone mountain country of Yugoslavia—the true karst—has been a favourite hunting ground for speleologists for well over a century. The famous stalactite Caves of Postojna, with their electric railway, though known in the Middle Ages, were not fully explored and developed until 1818, but since then have attracted hundreds of thousands of visitors every year. Caving in Yugoslavia, as in neighbouring Italy and Austria, is very much more than a mere sport, and karst science and speleology are standard university subjects, adjuncts to the more general courses on geology.

Bulgaria and Rumania both have a number of limestone caves, especially in the Rumanian Carpathians round Cluj. The Adam Cave in the Dobruja is particularly famous, containing some fine remains of prehistoric animals.

Austria's Eisriesenwelt—over 25 miles of stupendous ice caverns—in the Tennengebirge near Salzburg, is, like Postojna, one of the marvels of Europe. Elsewhere in Austria, some of the gigantic caves of the Northern and Southern Limestone Alps are well over 1,500 feet deep; while for the curious visitor the Dürrnberg salt mines at Hallein provide an interesting two-hour tour of a subterranean world dating back to Neolithic times, the deepest point being 1,500 feet below ground. A similar excursion can be made of the Hallstatt salt mines in the Dachstein range, where relics of Stone Age culture have also been found.

In Switzerland, the world's second longest cave system, the Hölloch, near Lucerne, has now been explored for almost 65 miles. The deepest limestone cave in the country is the Gouffre du Chevrier in the canton of Vaud (1,654 feet). Caves such as the Drachenloch and Wildmannlisloch have yielded relics of prehistoric bear cults.

Germany too provides excellent opportunities for the caver and prehistorian, especially in the Swabian and Franconian Alps. The Bärenhöhle and Nebelhöhle are among the best known in the Swabian Alps, the former for its remains of cave bears, the latter so named after the grey mist that occasionally belches out—actually warm air flowing from the interior when the outside temperature drops below that of the cave. The labyrinthine passages of the extensive Klutert Cave system were used as air raid shelters in the second World War, and the Cavern of Barbarossa in the Harz Mountains, with an area of 27,000 square yards, is one

of the largest in Germany. The country also has a spectacular ice cave, the Schellenberg Cavern in Bavaria.

Poland has large caves in the High Tatras, one of them, the Sniezna, ranking with the world's deepest (2,034 feet). Among the karst caves of Czechoslovakia is the Demanova Cave, six storeys deep, with galleries totalling twelve and a half miles. There are many such caves on the frontier with Hungary, and on the Hungarian side, but stretching below the border, is the entrance to the famous stalactitic Aggtalek Cave.

Although caving in the Soviet Union is not a notably popular recreational activity, there is much scientific study of karstic caves and their related problems. Some stalactite caves and potholes in the Caucasus are over 900 feet deep and the Red Cave system in the Crimea is about seven and a half miles long. Near Tarnapol there are enormous gypsum caves, one of them sixteen miles in length, unequalled anywhere. Prehistoric remains have been found in many regions, such as Uzbekistan and Siberia, and there are ice caves within the Arctic Circle.

Northern Europe, including Scandinavia, has its limestone areas, but the caves are in general smaller than those of the central European mountain ranges. In the Belgian Ardennes, however, the Grotte de Han is one of Europe's finest show caves, with the River Lesse coursing through the stalactite-filled caverns into an enormous, shimmering underground lake.

Caving in Britain

The limestone caves of the British Isles offer considerable scope and

Tourists in the Mammoth Cave, Kentucky.

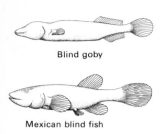

Blind goby

Mexican blind fish

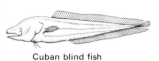

Cuban blind fish

Blind cave fishes from Kentucky and Mexico.

A cave under the principal Maya pyramid of Chichén Itzá once contained sacrificial remains, including humans.

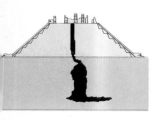

challenge for potholers even if they do not rank with the greatest in the world. The traditional caving regions are in Derbyshire, Yorkshire, the Mendip Hills of Somerset and South Wales; but other areas such as Devon, Furness in the Lake District, North Wales and the Scottish Highlands also have their enthusiastic devotees.

It was in the Yorkshire dales that British speleologists set the pace after the first descent of Gaping Gill by Edouard-Alfred Martel in 1895. The main chamber of this pothole (about 500 feet long, 90 feet wide and 110 feet high) is the largest in Britain. Yorkshire also has what is described as the most difficult cave system in the country, at Mossdale. Like others in the area, it is liable to sudden flooding and in 1967 claimed the lives of six cavers. The most famous and deepest pothole in the country is Penyghent Pot (527 feet).

Derbyshire's Peak District has a rich variety of potholes and caves. Nettle Pot is very nearly as deep as Gaping Gill and is notoriously difficult to negotiate. Eldon Hole has also represented a challenge to cavers for centuries. It has been claimed, though not proved, that the 200-foot shaft was descended in Elizabeth I's reign.

South Wales can currently claim both the longest and deepest cave systems in Britain, only successfully explored in recent years. Ogof Agen Allwedd has passages that extend to more than fourteen miles and still offers tremendous opportunities for cavers. So too does Ogof Ffynnon Ddu, which is about 800 feet deep, with intermediate parts only accessible to divers.

In the Mendips, the most celebrated tourist attraction is Wookey Hole, a splendid show cave consisting of three chambers, an under-

ground river and archaeological finds dating back 60,000 years. Other submerged chambers are still being explored by divers. Swildon's Hole is another wonderful cave system, where exploration began at the start of this century and still continues. Here again the farthest reaches are accessible only to divers. Even more complicated, by reason of its maze of passages (not for nothing is part of it called the Rabbit Warren), is St Cuthbert's Swallet, classified as one of the very difficult caves in the area.

Devon too has its show caves, the most celebrated of which is Kent's Cavern near Torquay, with animal and human remains extending back to the Stone Age.

Scotland's limestone caves are mainly confined to Sutherland, and Fingal's Cave in the Inner Hebrides, composed of basalt lava and formed by wave action, is world famous, thanks to the composer Mendelssohn.

Ireland has already proved to be prolific in limestone caves. More than 300 have been explored in the southern and northwestern counties and clearly this is a region of considerable interest for all enterprising potholers.

Marvels of the New World

In the United States, the majority of the famous caves are situated in the central, western and south-western states. The chief exceptions are the vast cave systems of Kentucky. The Flint Ridge Caves are now explored to a total distance of over 72 miles, while the neighbouring Mammoth Cave system is only about ten miles shorter. The stalactites in the five-storey Mammoth Cavern are perhaps the most sensational in the world. To the north, the Blue Spring Cave, with almost nineteen miles of passages mapped, now ranks among the world's "top ten". Another showplace farther east is Virginia's Luray Cavern, discovered in 1878, which contains a beautiful array of dripstone wonders, including an organ, the pipes of which are made of stalactites.

Most of the other great caves are situated farther west. The Jewel Cave and Wind Cave in South Dakota are both protected national monuments. The latter is over 30 miles long, the fifth longest in the world.

New Mexico has many marvellous caves for the visitor, of which the fantastic Carlsbad Caverns are the most renowned. Its Big Room is the largest cave on earth, at 33 miles it is the fourth longest system in the country and it is also the deepest (1,320 feet) in the United States. In this state too are the famous Gila Cliff Dwellings, rivalled by those of the Mesa Verde in Colorado. The Timpanogos Cave in Utah and the Lehman Caves in Nevada are also open to the public as national monuments.

The deepest cave in the New World—to date—is in Mexico, the Sotano del San Agustin (2,008 feet), and another, the Cueva de Rio Iglesia, runs it very close. In the Cueva Chica, near San Luis Potosi, lives the blind cave fish *Anoptichthys jordani*. Well preserved carvings and paintings from Olmec times, about 2,500 years ago, have been found in the caves of Juxtahuaca in the state of Guerrero.

Africa, Asia and Australasia

In Africa, there are karst regions in Morocco and Algeria, partially explored, and cave areas in Central Africa which are hardly known. South Africa has a number of show caves which are both beautiful and of importance to palaeontologists. Madagascar has some well explored cave systems, the largest to date having been traced for more than two miles.

In the Middle East, Lebanon's Jeita Cave, with its subterranean river, is outstanding. The Holy Land too conceals much history underground. The caves of Mount Carmel in Israel have yielded Stone Age relics more than 100,000 years old, while the caves of the Wadi Qumran in Jordan, on the Dead Sea, have harboured Biblical scrolls that have proved to be the earliest Old Testament manuscripts yet discovered.

In the Himalayas, Malaya, Thailand, Vietnam and Indonesia, there are caves of great splendour and prehistoric interest, while China, with its enormous limestone regions, has many thousands of caves, including those at Chou-Kou-Tien, where the remains of *Sinanthropus* were found. Japan has some lovely caves on the island of Honshu, and there are lava caves in the shadow of Mount Fujiyama.

Finally, there are the stalactite caves of western and southeastern Australia, the dry caves of the Nullabor Plain, and the volcanic caves of New Zealand, including the celebrated "glow-worm" grotto of Waitomo.

Caves in South Africa revealed fossil remains of the most primitive type of hominid yet discovered, Australopithecus.

Gypsum crystals in the Cottonwood Cave.

A GLOSSARY OF
CAVING TERMS

Abseil   A method of rapidly descending steep pitches by means of a double rope.

Active cave or system   A cave or caves still being enlarged by water.

Acetylene lamp   A miner's lamp lit by burning acetylene gas, produced by the action of water on calcium carbide. Also called carbide lamp.

Anemolite   A stalactite showing erratic growth away from the vertical, with branches curving and twisting in many directions. Also called eccentric or helictite.

Anthodite   A type of cave flower formed from crystals of gypsum or aragonite.

Aragonite   Crystalline form of calcium carbonate, mainly precipitated from hot springs.

Bed   A layer or stratum in a belt of sedimentary rock.

Bedding plane   A separation line between two layers of rock. Also a low passage in same.

Belay (Noun)   A point at which a rope, ladder or climber can be anchored to a rock. (Verb) The act of attaching oneself, a rope or a ladder to a rock anchorage.

Belay length   A short length of rope utilized for a belay. Also known simply as a belay.

Bivouac   A temporary camp in a long-distance cave expedition.

Boulder choke   A pile of rocks or boulders, as from a collapsed roof, often blocking further passage.

Breccia   Limestone fragments, often angular in shape, deposited in caves due to faulting, erosion, etc.

Bridge   A rock wedge or arch spanning a passage.

Calcareous   Formed from, containing, or related to, calcium carbonate deposits.

Calcite   Calcium carbonate in crystallized form, the main constituent of limestone.

Carbide lamp   A lamp much used by cavers, with a flame produced by burning acetylene gas. Also called acetylene lamp.

Even in active, water-filled caves thick, sticky mud may be deposited in quiet stretches of water.

The Hall of the Titans in the Eiskogel Cave.

Dried out and cracked cave mud.

Cascade A calcite formation resembling a frozen waterfall.

Cave A natural underground cavity, formed by the action of water, lava, wind, waves, ice, etc.

Cave deposit Debris on the floor of a cave, such as clay, gravel, silt, sand or fossils.

Cave pearl A smooth, circular piece of calcite or aragonite, formed by the rotating water action around a nucleus, such as a grain of sand.

Caver A person who visits and explores caves for sport or scientific research, a speleologist. Sometimes called a potholer or spelunker (U.S.).

Cave system A large, complex arrangement of passages, shafts and chambers.

Chamber A large hall-like cavern, opening out from a passage or shaft.

Chimney A narrow, vertical or steeply inclined fissure.

Chockstone A rock wedged in a crack, capable of being used as a belay point.

Clinometer A surveying instrument for measuring angles of dip or slope.

A carbide (acetylene) lamp.

Clint The corroded surface of limestone outcrops, characterized by criss-cross grooves.

Column A pillar-like formation linking cave roof and floor, usually as a result of a joined stalactite and stalagmite.

Corrasion The wearing away of rock by the abrasive action of particles in fast-flowing water.

Corrosion The chemical dissolution of rock by water containing carbonic acid.

Crawl A low passage through which progress can only be made on hands and knees, or flat-out.

Current mark Hollow or fluted mark on cave walls or floor, caused by fast-flowing water. Also called scallop or flow marking.

Curtain A thin, fluted sheet or draping of dripstone; sometimes a row or group of regularly-shaped stalactites.

Dark zone The part of a cave not reached by natural light.

Dig An excavation above or below ground to find a new cave or section of cave.

Dip The inclination of a bed of rock, its angle from the horizontal being expressed in degrees. It is measured by a clinometer.

Doline Surface hollow caused by solution or by the collapse of an underlying cave.

Dolomite Carbonate of calcium and magnesium, occurring in sedimentary beds.

Drag stretcher A specially designed stretcher, used in cave rescues.

Dripstone Rock formations built up by continuously dripping or seeping ground water.

Duck A point where the roof slopes to meet the water level, or where there is little air space, traversed by a quick duck or dive, to emerge on the other side.

Eccentric An irregularly shaped dripstone formation.

Electron ladder A lightweight ladder made of wire, with metal rungs.

Erosion The wearing away of rock by physical or chemical action.

Etrier A small section of ladder which can be roped to another and extended as required.

Exposure Bodily deterioration, sometimes resulting in death, caused by extreme wet and cold conditions, or by lack of food and water.

Exposure suit A specially designed suit for keeping the body warm and dry.

Fault A line of fracture in a rock, caused by movement of the earth's crust.

Fissure A narrow, vertical break or cave passage.

Flow marking Alternative term for current mark or scallop.

Flowstone A continuous sheet of calcite, covering a cave wall or floor.

Fluorescein A harmless green dye, used for tracing underground water and its points of emergence.

Formation Any decorative cave deposit, including stalactites, stalagmites and helictites.

Gallery A high passage linking two parts of a cave system.

Gour A rimstone pool formed by deposits of calcite.

Grike A deep groove or fissure in clints.

Grotto A small chamber or cave, often illuminated in a show cave.

Gypsum Hydrous calcium sulphate.

Helictite A stalactite showing erratic growth. Also called eccentric or anemolite.

Heligmite A stalagmite showing erratic, branching growth.

Hydrology The scientific study of underground water and water courses.

Joint A division, often vertical, through a bed of rock. A joint traversing several beds is a master joint.

Karabiner A metal snap link used for fastening ropes to belays, connecting ladders, etc.

Karst A limestone region, such as in northern Yugoslavia, where the rapid drainage of rain water underground creates many caves.

Letterbox A narrow slit in a rock.

Lifeline A safety rope, fixed in various ways, to protect a caver in ascents, descents and difficult or dangerous climbing operations.

Limestone Sedimentary rock containing calcium carbonate, ideal for the formation of caves.

Master cave The main cave in a system, where passages converge.

Pitted clints in Dachstein limestone.

Clints in limestone outcrops.

125

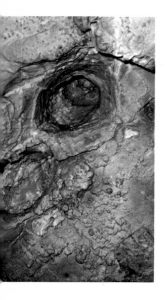

Holes in the roof caused by corrosion.

Maypole A scaling pole constructed from short sections and held by guylines, used to reach higher passages.

Moonmilk A soft calcite deposit, thought to be caused by bacterial action.

Phreatic cave A cave formed in the waterlogged zone, below the water table.

Pitch A vertical section of cave, usually requiring the use of a ladder.

Piton A steel spike, driven into a rock crack to provide a belay or foothold.

Pothole A vertical shaft, either open to the sky or inside a cave.

Prusik A technique of rope ascent, using sling stirrups and sliding knots.

A stream of visitors in the Mammoth Cave.

Reptation Progress through a tight passage by crawling or squeezing, reptile-like.

Resurgence The main point at which underground water emerges at the surface, as in a spring.

Rimstone pool A small basin with a calcareous edge formed by thin films of flowing water.

Rising A point where underground water rises to the surface.

Rockmill A hole in the bed of a stream, caused by rotating stones.

Scallop A hollow mark on a rock wall or floor caused by the force of water. Also called current mark or flow marking.

Shaft The vertical entrance to a mine or pothole.

Sinkhole A place where water sinks or has once sunk underground.

Sinter A calcite cave formation such as a stalactite or stalagmite.

Siphon A place in a cave passage where water ebbs and flows in a siphoning action; also applied generally to a flooded section.

Speleology The exploration and scientific study of caves.

Spelunker American term for a caver.

Squeeze A narrow cave opening, just large enough for a human body to wriggle through.

Stalactite A formation, usually of calcite, hanging from a cave roof.

Stalagmite A formation, usually of calcite, growing from a cave floor.

Stemple A wood or metal wedge designed to be used as a ladder or for hoisting a load.

Straw stalactite A thin, hollow, regularly-shaped stalactite.

Strike A horizontal line of a bedding plane at right angles to the true dip.

Sump A point in a cave where water prevents further exploration, often the end of a cave. Short sumps can be negotiated by free or equipped diving.

Swallet The opening in limestone rock where a stream vanishes underground.

Swallow hole An opening through which a stream flows underground.

Tail The loose end of a ladder beyond the final rung, used for connecting with another ladder.

Threshold The entrance to a cave or pothole as far as the natural light extends.

Trap A place where the cave roof dips under water, and shortly re-emerges.

Traverse (Noun) A horizontal climb along a ledge or between the walls above the floor of a passage. (Verb) To move in a horizontal direction, especially along a high ledge.

Troglobite A creature that lives permanently in the dark zone of caves.

Troglophile A species found both in and outside caves. Specimens living in the dark zone of caves sometimes complete their life cycle there.

Trogloxene An animal that occasionally enters a cave but is not a permanent resident.

Tube An almost circular cave passage.

Tufa or tuff A calcareous deposit in limestone or in caves.

Vadose cave A cave formed above the waterlogged zone, or water table.

Waistlength A length of safety rope attached round the waist, which can be connected by a lifeline or belay point.

Water table The upper surface of the waterlogged or phreatic zone of the earth's crust.

This collecting jar placed beneath a stalactite was covered with white limestone after only three months.

The Insuyu Cave in Turkey has splendid stalactite decorations and a cave lake.

FURTHER READING

Barrington, Nicholas & Stanton; William, *The Complete Caves of Mendip*, Barton Publications, 1970.

Bögli, A. & Franke, H. W., *Darkness, the Wonderful World of Caves*, Rand McNally, 1967.

Casteret, Norbert, *Ten Years Under the Earth*, J. M. Dent, 1939.

Casteret, Norbert, *The Darkness Under the Earth*, J. M. Dent, 1954.

Cave Research Group of Great Britain, *British Caving*, Routledge & Kegan Paul, 1962.

Cons, David, *Cavecraft*, George G. Harrap, 1966.

Cullingford, C. H. D., *Exploring Caves*, Oxford University Press, 1951.

Ford, Trevor, *The Caves of Derbyshire*, Dalesman Publishing Co., 1965.

Grigson, Geoffrey, *Painted Caves*, Phoenix House, 1957.

Jasinski, Marc, *Caves and Caving*, Paul Hamlyn, 1967.

Jenkins, D. W. & Williams, Mason, *Caves in Wales and the Marches*, Dalesman Publishing Co., 1969.

Longsworth, P., *Exploring Caves*, T. Y. Crowell, 1959.

Lovelock, James, *Caving*, B. T. Batsford, 1969.

Lübke, Anton, *The World of Caves*, Weidenfeld & Nicolson, 1958.

Mohr, C. E. & Poulsons, T., *Life of the Cave*, McGraw-Hill, 1967.

Pond, A. W., *Caverns of the World*, Grosset & Dunlap, 1965.

Robinson, Donald, *Potholing and Caving*, Educational Productions, 1967.

Robinson, Donald & Greenbank, Anthony, *Caving and Potholing*, Constable, 1964.

Stenuit, Robert & Jasinski, Marc, *Caves and the Marvellous World Beneath Us*, Nicholas Vane and A. S. Barnes (U.S.), 1966.

Tazieff, Haroun, *Caves of Adventure*, Hamish Hamilton, 1953.

Thornber, Norman, *Pennine Underground*, Dalesman Publishing Co., 1965.

INDEX